LONDON SE7 8RE
TEL. NO. 081 319 2525

DESIGNS
ON
VICTORY

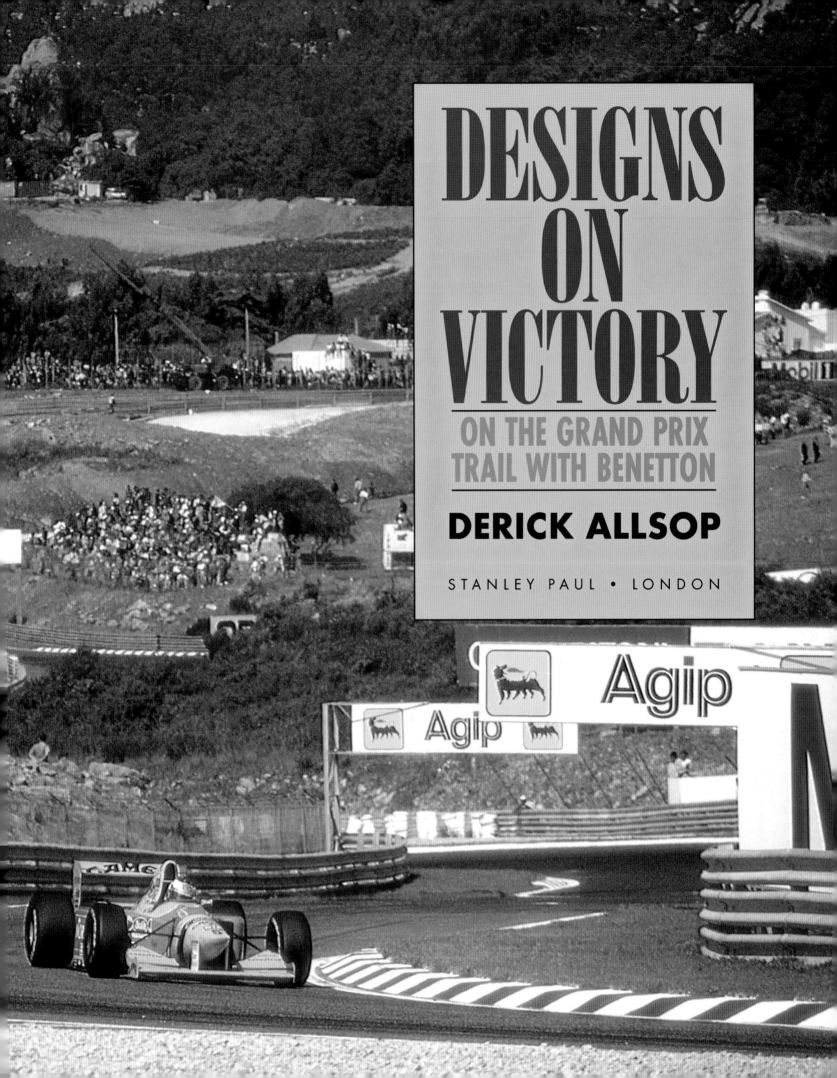

DESIGNS ON VICTORY

ON THE GRAND PRIX TRAIL WITH BENETTON

DERICK ALLSOP

STANLEY PAUL · LONDON

First published 1993

1 3 5 7 9 10 8 6 4 2

© Derick Allsop 1993

Derick Allsop has asserted his right under
the Copyright, Designs and Patents Act, 1988
to be identified as the author of this work

First published in the United Kingdom in 1993
by Stanley Paul Limited
Random House, 20 Vauxhall Bridge Road,
London SW1V 2SA

Random House Australia (Pty) Limited
20 Alfred Street, Milsons Point, Sydney,
New South Wales 2061, Australia

Random House New Zealand Limited
18 Poland Road, Glenfield,
Auckland 10, New Zealand

Random House South Africa (Pty) Limited
PO Box 337, Bergvlei, South Africa

Random House UK Limited Reg. No. 954009

A CIP catalogue record for this book is
available from the British Library

ISBN 0 09 178311 9

Set in Photina and Futura typefaces
Design/make-up by Roger Walker

Printed in Great Britain by
Butler & Tanner Ltd, Frome and London

Title page:
*A winding road to victory for Michael Schumacher at the
Portuguese Grand Prix*

To my team:
Sue, Natalie and Kate

ACKNOWLEDGEMENTS

Formula One motor racing is a team effort and so is this book. It would not have been possible without the generous assistance, co-operation and forbearance of the entire Camel Benetton Ford camp. I extend my sincere thanks to all concerned for allowing me on board to share their experiences on this journey through the past year. It would be remiss of me not to identify those who, in particular, have had to endure my presence and questions, and provided invaluable information and support: Luciano and Alessandro Benetton, Michael Schumacher, Riccardo Patrese, Flavio Briatore, Tom Walkinshaw, Ross Brawn, Rory Byrne, Gordon Message, Richard Grundy, Joan Villadelprat, Frank Dernie, Pat Symonds, Allan McNish, Stuart and Diana Spires, Andrew Alsworth, Kenny Handkammer, Wayne Bennett, Dave Hughes, Jon Harriss, Martin Pople, Kristan de Groot, Patrizia Spinelli, Rae Turkington, Rod Vickery, Antonella Bartoletti and Sally Poole; Steve Parker, Don Hume, Sophie Sicot and Steve Madincea, of Ford; Dick Scammell and Jim Brett, of Cosworth; Duncan Lee, Patricia Guerendel and Irene Macarty, of Camel; Maria Bellanca, Victoria Flack and colleges at Jardine PR; Martin Brundle, Alain Prost, Damon Hill and Willi Weber; and ever-trusty accomplices, Ann Bradshaw, Tim Collings, Niki Takeda, Stan Piecha, Ray Matts, Maurice Hamilton and Sue Allsop.

I wish, also, to acknowledge the rest of the Benetton cast: Harry Bevis, William Box, Ted Burden, Michael Chalk, Wendy Chard, Ian Douglas, Pam Dunnet, Annabelle Forer, Russell George, Graham Giles, Ted Gould, Terry Rogers, Maureen Ross, Jessica Salisbury, Robert Sprules, James Wright, Mark Faulkner, Michael Nolan, Andrew Saunders, Willem Toet, Nicholas Tombazis, Richard Washington, John Whyte, Les Young, Nigel Atkinson, John Barr, Steve Bates, Michael Buter, Ronnie Dean, Keith Dunsby, Philip Henderson, Steve Joyce, Steve Martin, Richard McNicholas, James Morris, Steven Morse, Paul Roberts, Adam Sharp, Graham Skelcher, Many Tansley, Alan Watts, Colin Watts, Stuart Webb, Shane West, Mick Wilkinson, Robert Williams, Ross Williams, Reece Witchell, Mick Bennett, Ian Burgin, Dave Hanna, Graham Heard, Nigel Jackson, Richard McAinsh, Brian McIlwaine, Andrew Moss, Gerard O'Flaherty, Mark Oxley, Dave Rensall, Tony Shrimpton, Alan Tagg, Martin Tolliday, Dave Wass, Michael Wilson, Andy Wymer, Rossella Panseri, David Ashton, Deana Clark, Tadeusz Czapski, Rob Gough, Richard Marshall, Alan Permane, Peter Scrimshaw, Paul Whiting, Christian Silk, Malcolm Tierney, Alan Bond, Ian Calcutt, David Cooper, Robin Grant, Chris Martin, Barrie McRoberts, Dave Miller and Andrew Poole.

Jonathan Briade, Rachael Gubbins, Suzanne Hanks, Jackie Stone, Marie Surman, Peter Metcalf, Grahame Snowden, Fred Mundle, Brian Andrews, Abdul Basher, Simon Biddle, Alex Fullerton, Ian Hudson, John Jordan, Terry Starling, Gary Andrews, David Bayliss, Dave Briggs, David Chalk, Jim Filmer, Jeff Fullerton, Pat Gee, Peter Green, Steve Green, Mark Hains, Trevor Kennerson, Steven Lapper, Steve Merchant, Steve Houlihan, Nigel Rowles, Simon Tiensa, Mark Townsend, Craig Ward, Pat Warner, Kevin Young, Michael Boon, Philip Hopping, Kevin Lee, Gian-Franco Cicogna, Sharon Deakin, Charlotte Hare, John Coppock, Paul Franklin, Michael Fuller, Chris Glass, Michael Hilder, Ian Hornby, John Mardle, Carolyn Morley, Keith Saunt, Alec Titchener, Glyn Beeby, Adrian Ward, Dave Hamer, Bill Millar, Mick Ainsley-Cowlishaw, Tim Baston, Robert Bushell, Dave Butterworth, Lee Calcutt, Max Fluckiger, Paul Howard, Michael Jakeman, Dave Jones, Steve Matchett, Dave Redding, Paul Seaby, Jonathan Wheatley, Dave Campbell, Simon Morley, David Sheard, Peter Aldridge, Ray Beasley, Steve Bird, Colin Butler, Barnie Drew-Smythe, Carl Gibson, Carlos Nunes, Mark Owen, Kim Phillips, Derek Rodgers, Chris Tuckey, Paul Wesson, Gerald Kerrison, Peter Williams, Neville Wood, Maria Minton and Keith Minton.

My final word of thanks goes to the man responsible for the pictures in this book. Steven Tee, of LAT, has, I believe, captured the spectacle and emotions of the sport as few can. His superb technique is matched by an uncanny perception and rare imagination.

CONTENTS

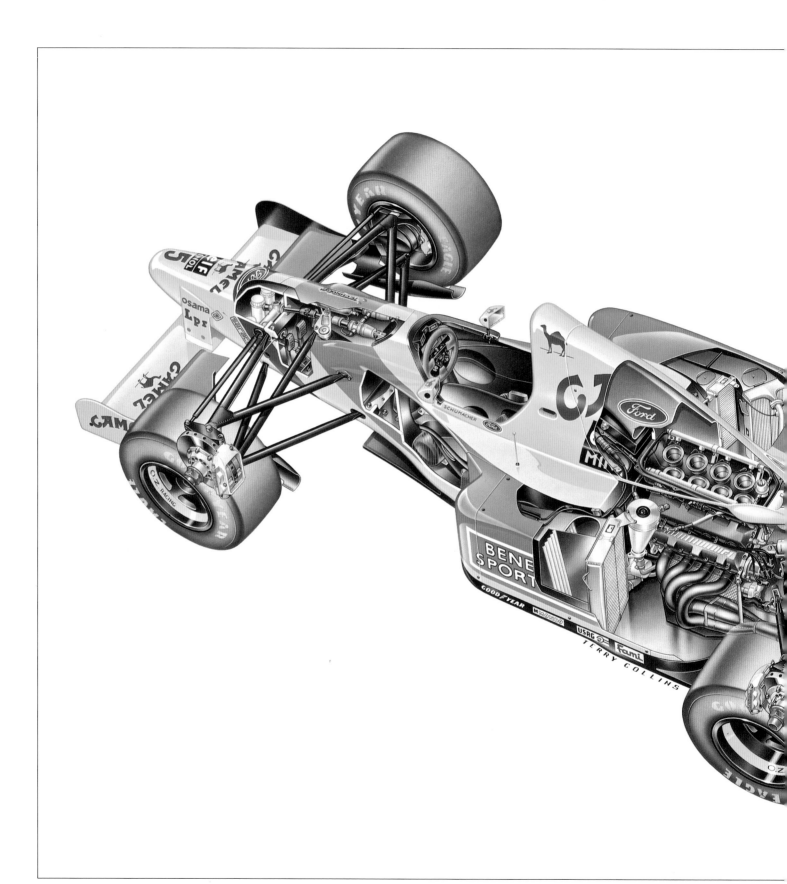

FOREWORD

It is with great pleasure that I welcome you all into our home at Camel Benetton Ford and hope that this book gives you a better understanding and appreciation of all the work and commitment that goes into our team operation. I believe it is important for you, the people who support motor racing, to be given an insight into life not only here at Benetton, but within Formula One as a whole.

I consider it very important to let people know what happens in Formula One. It is your sport as well as ours. Communications are vital to the future of the sport and the business. I believe that to take Formula One forward in the right direction we all have to be pulling together – drivers, team managers, mechanics, sponsors, the media and you, the public.

We at Benetton are still a relatively young team but I hope we are contributing to this cause. We have a talented, hard-working, enthusiastic team, and we are endeavouring to improve ourselves and the show. I trust the efforts of the people involved – and racing should be, above all, about people – will become more apparent as you read through this book.

Above: *Michael Schumacher, Flavio Briatore and Riccardo Patrese*
Opposite: *The Camel Benetton Ford B193B*

Flavio Briatore
Managing Director
Benetton Formula Ltd

INTRODUCTION

The men at Witney and Luciano Benetton had much in common. Ambitious, enterprising and determined, they were prepared to pit themselves against power, might and The Establishment. So it was that the humble English racing outfit drove through the ranks to reach Formula One status, and the Italian who delivered his sister's hand-knitted sweaters by bicycle rode to the top of the clothing trade.

Their paths crossed in 1985, when the then Toleman team took on board sponsorship from Benetton. That Toleman had survived at all in Grand Prix racing was a monumental achievement, given their early experience at this level.

Flavio Briatore and Derick Allsop

The climb from the European Formula Two Championship, which they dominated in 1980, to Formula One the following year proved, to put it mildly, hazardous. Many dismissed the attempt as foolhardy. Merely qualifying was beyond them at most of those early races. But they persisted with their cumbersome car, irreverently known as 'The Flying Pig', refined their act and eventually produced a Hart turbo-powered machine to be taken seriously. They were rewarded in 1983 with their first World Championship points, courtesy of Derek Warwick's fine drive in the Dutch Grand Prix, at Zandvoort. There wasn't a dry eye in the house.

Points flowed consistently for the rest of that season and, in 1984, a young Brazilian called Ayrton Senna entered Formula One with Toleman. By the end of the following season he had signed for Lotus and, acrimonious though the parting was, he had played his part in confirming Toleman's emergence as a force to be reckoned with.

Benetton, too, had begun to make their presence felt. In common with all Italian males, Luciano Benetton had a passion for racing cars and, in particular, for Ferrari. The company, established with his sister Giuliana, and his brothers Carlo and Gilberto, in the mid-1970s, ventured into Formula One as sponsors of Tyrrell, in 1983. They shared in Michele Alboreto's success at the Detroit Grand Prix that year. A spell with Alfa Romeo preceded the switch to Toleman.

This, though, was to be no flirtation with sponsorship. Benetton went one better by buying the whole operation and, at the start of 1986, Benetton Formula was born. Still based at Witney, Oxfordshire, the team had its first Grand Prix victory by the end of that year, Gerhard Berger coaxing the Benetton BMW turbo ahead of Prost, Senna, Piquet and Mansell in Mexico.

The team enjoyed further success in 1989 (Japan), 1990 (Japan and Australia), 1991 (Canada) and 1992 (Belgium). There were other significant landmarks. The team became Ford's flagship and demonstrated its intentions to compete at the highest level by signing up its own sponsors, Camel. The entire racing organisation was restructured, with Flavio Briatore, previously Commercial Director, moving up to Managing Director. Tom Walkinshaw, a man steeped in racing, was brought in as Engineering Director, while Ross Brawn became Technical Director. Alessandro Benetton, son of Luciano, is President and family figurehead of the racing team, which is now housed at a new, £12-million state-of-the-art factory near the Cotswold village of Enstone.

As the Benetton Group has grown in stature – it has interests in a wide range of sporting apparel, 7000 shops in more than 100 countries and an annual turnover of $2 billion – so Benetton Formula has established itself among the elite of Formula One. The target now is to reach the pinnacle of the sport.

This is the inside story of the team's relentless quest for ultimate success; an insight into the workings and emotions of not only Benetton but of Formula One as a whole; around the globe and around the calendar; week by week and race by race. Grand Prix racing has become both the test-bed and shop window of advanced technology. This, however, endeavours above all to relate the story of the people who weave the web of intrigue and fascination which beguiles billions of viewers every motor racing season.

Derick Allsop
Rochdale, Lancashire
England
October 1993

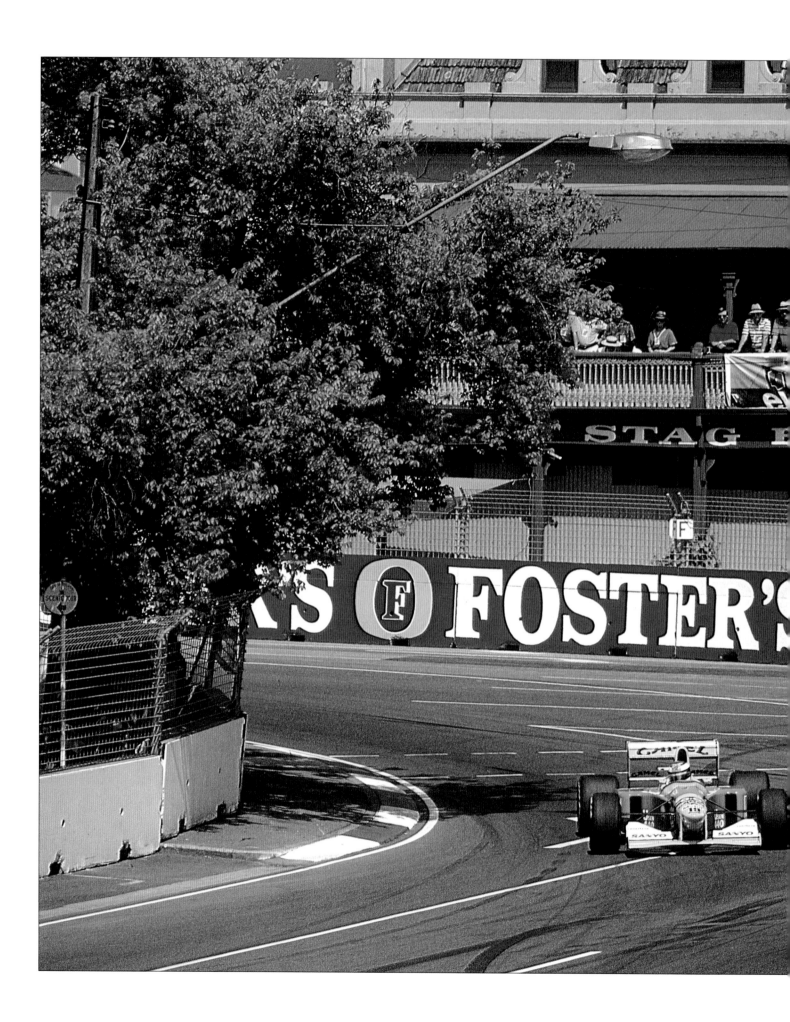

CHAPTER 1

WHAT BREAK?

Formula One is all things to all men: a sport or a business; a passion or a plaything; the supreme human and mechanical challenge, or an obscenely expensive irrelevance. To those involved it is an all-consuming job of work, the pursuit of excellence, a never-ending toil and commitment. There is always another trick to try, another avenue to investigate. Those who have neither the wit nor stamina to last the pace are left by the wayside.

Even as the Formula One show was completing its 1992 tour, in Japan and Australia, the troops back home were setting up a new base camp for Benetton Formula's assault on the 1993 World Championship and beyond. A huge factory near Enstone, a few miles north of the old spiritual home at Witney, would house the hopes and aspirations of the future.

Brundle applauds Japanese Grand Prix winner Patrese, his successor at Benetton

Facing page: Brundle shines to take third place in Japan

Within Formula One it was generally recognised that that future looked bright. The consistency of the Camel Benetton Fords, driven by the precocious German, Michael Schumacher, and the doughty Englishman, Martin Brundle, were jousting with the McLaren Hondas of Ayrton Senna and Gerhard Berger for second place in the Constructors' Championship as they headed for the final sector of the season. The title had long since been decided, Williams Renault wrapping it up back in Belgium.

In that race, at the spectacular Spa-Francorchamps circuit, 23-year-old Schumacher had registered his first Grand Prix win, just a year after making his Formula One debut on that very track. The Drivers' Championship had been secured by Nigel Mansell even earlier, but those ten points strengthened Schumacher's position in the struggle for second, third and fourth places with Senna and Riccardo Patrese, in the other Williams.

■ ■ ■

Suzuka, Japan, Hondaland. The car manufacturers and engine partners to McLaren have already announced their decision to 'suspend' their Formula One activities at the end of the season, so Benetton are bracing themselves for a massive offensive in this, the final appearance by Honda on home territory. Qualifying confirms Benetton's belief. The Williams pair, Mansell and Patrese, occupy their usual places at the front of the grid, but then come Senna and Berger, in the McLarens. Schumacher is next, while Brundle is down in 13th place, the victim of food poisoning and a heavy shunt. Torrential rain on the second day washes away any prospect of a change to the order yet at least gives Brundle the opportunity to stay in bed.

Those who have queued out in the open all night are rewarded with a bright, sunny, warm race day. The Japanese are gripped in an almost hypnotic spell by

Formula One and, by first light, Suzuka is packed. Brundle, still groggy, decides to give himself a try in warm-up. He's eighth quickest, good enough to convince him he should race.

Schumacher's race lasts only 12 laps. He is running third when his gearbox fails him. Brundle, though, stays the course and comes in an excellent third, behind Patrese and Berger. The result virtually assures Patrese the runner-up place in the Championship, while Senna remains three points ahead of Schumacher. McLaren are now eight points clear of Benetton in the Constructors' table.

The Formula One wagon train reaches its last watering hole in a corner of South Australia. Adelaide was always generally regarded as a fairly sedate, dignified sort of place. You wouldn't have found anything like the brashness of Sydney or Melbourne here. Since 1985, however, Adelaide has gone through something of a personality change. For a week of the year, at any rate. Hosting the final Grand Prix of the season has seen to that.

Australians put on a party better than most. They also go about their sport with more vigour than most. Give them the opportunity of combining the two and you have an unbridled jamboree, the perfect end-of-term release for the teams. Little wonder it has become the favourite race of the year.

From a driver's point of view, Adelaide offers more scope and opportunities than the average street circuit. It is a severe challenge when weather conditions are good. Grip is at a premium and even the extremely gifted have come to grief on these slippery corners. When it rains here, conditions are impossible. The drivers had to endure torrential rain in 1989. They described it variously as 'a nightmare', 'a fiasco' and 'madness'. Two years later the deluge was worse still and the organisers called a merciful halt after 14 laps, making it the shortest race in the history of the World Championship.

Delight for Schumacher

The weather on this 1992 race day, 8 November, is uncertain. The air is fresh, the skies have become overcast. The local forecasters, though, are optimistic that we may just avoid another downpour.

Mansell and Senna cannot avoid each other after 19 laps at the front of the field, much to the anger of the Englishman, who had craved a 10th win of the season before seeking pastures new in IndyCars. When Patrese, too, goes, only Berger's McLaren is running ahead of Schumacher and Brundle.

Thirty of the 81 laps remain and Schumacher is trailing by 22 seconds. Of course he'll give it a go, but he is confronted by traffic. The Austrian is getting away. Suddenly Michael is on to a clear stretch of road. He posts a succession of fastest lap times – five of them in eight laps – to eat into Berger's advantage.

Could it also be that the McLaren Honda is down on fuel?

Schumacher sustains his astonishing attack to the line but Berger has done just enough. He wins by eight-tenths of a second. Schumacher, though, had produced the outstanding drive of the day to finish second and edge out Senna for third place in the Drivers' table, behind Mansell and Patrese. The dependable Brundle is third, to complete another splendid day for the Camel Benetton Ford camp. The team are third in the final Constructors' standings, a remarkable 70 points above fourth-placed Ferrari. What's more, they have become the first team in modern times to have scored points in every race of the Championship.

Grand finale... Benetton's Brundle and Schumacher flank race-winner Berger on the Adelaide podium

Schumacher's huge smile – a welcome feature of 1992 – is evident again. 'If you had told me at the beginning of the season, my first full season in Formula One, that I would finish third in the Championship, I would not have believed you,' he says. 'I am so happy.'

He is entitled to be happy. So are the rest of the Benetton team. They have done a fine job, not only here this weekend, but around the world at 16 different racing venues. The handshakes and back-slapping in the garage represent one kind of ritual celebration and self-congratulation. Come the evening, the equipment cleared and the last piece of data logged, it's appropriate to indulge in another kind. It's time, as they say, to party.

All over Adelaide, in public bars, in private clubs, even in the streets, they're bopping and firing back the amber nectar. The Camel bash is reckoned to be one of the best in town.

'I suppose you're looking forward to a nice long break now,' enquires a local innocent of an engineer clinging to his can.

The response is delivered with a wry grin. 'Break? What break?'

CHAPTER 2

WINTER WONDERLAND

For some, of course, mainly those in the racing crew, this is the best chance to take a holiday, catch up on the decorating that has been put off all year or simply re-acquaint themselves with the family. Back at the Benetton factory, though, they're busy moving in and adjusting to new surroundings while keeping the wheels of production turning and maintaining the momentum of the season just completed.

The spotlight of the Grand Prix is as distant as Australia itself. In any case, Adelaide and 1992 have gone. All the activity here is being channelled towards the next challenge and the next season: to 1993. Flavio Briatore, Tom Walkinshaw, Ross Brawn and Rory Byrne have set out their engineering and technical plan. Development work at the factory will run in parallel with a test programme out on the track.

Benetton, in common with most of the British-based Formula One teams, will be frequent visitors to Silverstone, the nation's regular Grand Prix circuit, through the winter months. It has the necessary facilities, provides a realistic gauge to progress and is convenient. Benetton also make use of the strip at RAF Kemble, mainly for systems checks and more basic testing.

Flavio Briatore, Managing Director of Benetton Formula Ltd, in his office

British winters are not, however, the most accommodating and Benetton join the frequent flyers down into Europe in search of more clement conditions. Estoril, home of the Portuguese Grand Prix, holds several test sessions during winter. The weather is not always dependable but the chances are it will be better than you'll find at Silverstone. The track is also varied and challenging, providing important information for drivers and teams.

A thorough test programme is vital for any team aspiring to the forefront of the sport. Many of the small, under-financed teams will remain off the pace because they do not have the means to prepare as well as they know they should. Benetton are among the more fortunate. They have sound backing and will embark upon an exhaustive winter test schedule.

■   ■   ■

29 November, Heathrow Airport, and familiar faces appear in the departure lounge. Destination: Lisbon. 'Here we go again,' says one.

Most teams employ separate test crews because the burden of 30 test sessions as well as 16 races would be too much. But there is an inevitable overlapping. Some engineers or technicians may be required for their particular skills and experience at particular tests. Many teams also appoint test drivers. Alessandro Zanardi, an Italian, will be on duty for Benetton at Estoril this week, along with Michael Schumacher and his new racing partner, Riccardo Patrese, who replaces Martin Brundle.

Benetton are stepping into the minefield of advanced technology, acknowledging that this is the only way forward. Their package for 1992 was effective and reliable. They demonstrated what could be achieved with a sensible, conventional concept, built around the neat and equally effective and reliable Ford Cosworth V8 engine. To tilt at the major prize they must take on board some of the myriad computer-controlled devices already mastered by Williams and known to be on the way at McLaren.

Gordon Message, Benetton's bearded team manager, leans on the pit wall at Estoril during one of the seemingly endless lulls in activity. 'What we did this year was show what can be done with good organisation and a bit of common sense,'

Designing the future of Benetton

he says in characteristically unpretentious manner.

Message was with the team back in their Toleman days. Before that, he was a mechanic with March. He has worked his way through the ranks yet taken on no airs or graces along the way. Perish the thought. He has a last draw on his cigarette, stamps it out and makes for the garage. He wouldn't be on a short-list for Benetton fashion models, but he is a model pro, as they'll tell you in the pit lane.

'He's a straight up-and-down bloke,' says one mechanic. 'He's basically still one of the lads. You know where you stand with him. That's the way it should be. There are too many posers in this game.'

Praise doesn't come much higher than that.

Rain is sweeping across the circuit and the nearby twin resorts of Estoril and Cascais on the second morning of the test. Enormous Atlantic rollers savage the coastline. So much for the clement conditions.

Many of the drivers, including Alain Prost, the new No. 1 at Williams, are reluctant to venture out. They kick around their garages, collars up, hands plunged deep into pockets. 'We might as well have been at Silverstone,' suggests one of the lads.

The sound of the rain, pattering on the pit lane, is drowned by the thunder of a firing engine. Heads pop out of the garages like rabbits from burrows. 'Wouldn't you know? It's Schumacher,' declares a self-appointed spokesman in a neighbouring pit.

Chuckles all round. And yet there is a grudging respect in the tone of the statement. Schumacher has a reputation for being a charger and for being

Tip of the iceberg... Benetton's factory at Enstone

Right: More like an operating theatre... the composites clean room

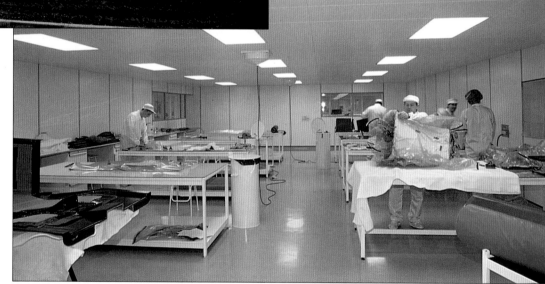

fearless. Perhaps too much of a charger and too fearless for his own good, some say. But there isn't a team in Formula One who wouldn't have him in their car. He is an exceptional talent, widely regarded as the best to emerge since Senna.

While others are cowering, Schumacher has work to do. He is testing the ABS braking system. Massive plumes of spray pursue the yellow and green car down the pit straight. When the rain relents and the track dries, he has the opportunity to make a valid comparison. 'The ABS is good in the wet, but it does not work so well in the dry,' he concludes with typical precision.

Schumacher is also anxious to compare the conventional, or passive, car with the car fitted with active suspension, the type of device which contributed so much to Williams' performance during 1992. Yes, he felt, the active was a distinct improvement.

Patrese begins work mid-week. He may be the most experienced driver in the history of the World Championship, with 240 appearances to date, but he is ill at ease reverting to a manual gear-box after growing used to Williams' semi-automatic transmission.

'I have come here to get to know the people and be close to the active programme,' says the 38-year-old Italian. 'My interest is in developing the active and traction control.'

Testing can be as teasing as it is tedious. Hour after hour, lap after lap of trying this, experimenting with that. Teams log opponents' times as well as their own. To no one's surprise, Williams are on top all week, with Damon Hill, the test driver still hoping to land the No. 2 job, slightly quicker than Prost, who admits he is still bedding in after a year's sabbatical.

Light and space... here in the race shop

Much of the attention is focused on the new team, Sauber. Most people regard the team as Mercedes, the engine Ilmor. The Swiss-based operation, headed by Peter Sauber, maintain they are Sauber, nothing more, nothing less. They have two talented drivers, the Finn, J. J. Lehto and the Austrian, Karl Wendlinger, who graduated from the Mercedes school with Schumacher.

Wendlinger posts a time of 1 minute 14.96 seconds, only 1.3 seconds slower than Hill's best. Lehto goes better still: 1 minute 14.33 seconds. What does Schumacher, with 1:15.69 in the active Benetton, make of that? 'Quick,' he says.

The problem with all these times, however, is that no team can be sure what their neighbours are up to, what their objectives are, what sort of fuel load they have and so on. Test team managers and drivers are constantly wondering how much significance they should attach to these times, and whether they are following the right trail.

This winter wonderland has many scenes. You'll find it at the old French Grand Prix circuit at Paul Ricard, near the medieval village of Le Castellet. Some will head for the Spanish Grand Prix circuit of Barcelona. Ferrari have their own test track, at Fiorano, and often pop down the road to Imola, home of the San Marino Grand Prix. Magny-Cours, home of the French Grand Prix now, is also the home of Ligier Renault so, naturally, they get through most of their test work there.

Pre-Christmas testing at Paul Ricard reinforces Schumacher's confidence in the active car but does little to comfort Patrese as he continues to wrestle with the conventional gearbox.

Come the next Estoril test, in January, the Camel Benetton Fords are nearing the specification the drivers can expect for the start of the season and Schumacher is positively ebullient. He splits the Williams pair, using an active car but a manual gearbox. He is within two-tenths of a second of Prost and six-hundredths of a second quicker than Hill, confirmed as Williams' second driver. 'We have made a lot of progress and the active suspension feels very good,' says the now 24-year-old German.

Patrese, however, is still having problems. His car has active suspension and semi-automatic transmission. 'We seem to have an imbalance and haven't yet reached any conclusion as to what the problem is,' says Ross Brawn.

■ ■ ■

The puzzle still unsolved, Alessandro Zanardi is summoned to Silverstone on 4 February to help find the answer. 'It's one of those niggling mysteries you get from

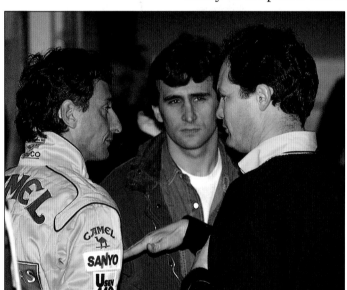

Test talk... Patrese, Zanardi and Dernie

Facing page: Wet, grey and desolate... the essence of winter testing

time to time,' says Gordon Message, standing at the counter of the circuit canteen. Silverstone Sid, legendary hands-on guardian, controller and surveyor of all that lives, breathes and happens here, is at a table, tucking into something which apparently demands his undivided attention.

A woman appears at the other side of the counter struggling with a large cardboard box. Message reaches over, takes it and makes for the door. 'Got to get the boys their breakfast,' he says.

The boys have the luxury of eating their breakfast at leisure. It is a bleak English morning right out of a 1950s B film: foggy, damp, chilly, unforgiving. They won't be rushing to get Zanardi out in these conditions. 'People get impatient, standing around, but there's no point going out when it's like this,' reasons Message. 'If it gets no better we'll do just a couple of laps later on to make sure the cars are okay.'

The shutters of the Benetton garage come down to signify an early lunch. 'Better go and find out what the boys want from the canteen,' says Message.

Come the afternoon the fog lifts sufficiently for Zanardi to run, and eventually some light is thrown on the problem. It's the software. Ah, that.

Twenty-four hours later Zanardi announces he has a racing job, with Lotus Ford.

■ ■ ■

Flavio Briatore is late to the office on 10 February, even though he has had what he describes as 'an early wake-up call'. A bomb had exploded outside his London home at 5.17 that morning. The device blew off the front door, destroyed one of the two pillars supporting the portico and smashed windows at the Grade II listed

building in Belgravia. Briatore, unhurt, says: 'I was sleeping and then there was a big explosion. I thought maybe it was a plane crashing. I was lucky.'

The following day Briatore presents a statement from the IRA, claiming responsibility. Police are working on the theory that the device was abandoned by an IRA bomber.

Briatore is at the centre of an explosive political situation within Formula One. Benetton and another team, Minardi, have so far declined to support a proposal to allow Williams into the 1993 Championship. The champions were 24 hours late with their application for entry and now require the 100 per cent backing of the other teams. Benetton feel Williams have obstructed genuine attempts to contain the development of technology, reduce costs and make Grand Prix racing more entertaining. Without the mandatory 100 per cent vote, nothing has been able to move. Briatore is turning Williams' own weaponry on them. He contends this stance is necessary to gain reform and a change to the system of reform.

Now Briatore is calling for an immediate cost-cutting exercise: a reduction in practice time, use of spare car, and the number of tyres and engines available to each team. Longer term, he urges, Formula One must rein back technology. 'We do not want to see Frank Williams' team out of the Championship but does he not see that if we do not do this there will be no Formula One World Championship in two or three years?' he warns.

He believes Benetton now have the credibility and stature to champion the cause of all the teams. This is an organisation with a firm infrastructure. If their involvement in Formula One ceases, the new factory will not be a white elephant. 'This technical facility is suitable for any of our other activities in Benetton Sportsystem,' he says with a distinctively Italian hunch of the shoulders and facial expression.

He lists the names under the Benetton Sportsystem banner as if reading from an autocue: 'Nordica, Prince, Asolo, Kastle, Rollerblade, Nitro, Langert, Grayfalloy, Ektelon and Killer Loop'. Those interests embrace the production of equipment for skiing, tennis, squash, badminton, golf, skating and mountain biking.

Briatore is perched on the edge of the desk in his spacious office. He is, as ever, impeccably attired. Behind him stand two elegant bookcases. Are those really books, or… ? Never mind. It's all very nice.

So is the factory. The white, 85,000 square foot building has been sunk into a 17-acre site to comply with planning regulations in this rural area. It is barely visible from the road. The workers have dubbed it 'The Iceberg'. The nine-tenths below ground level provides the latest in high-tech equipment. The whole factory

Schumacher's commercial break

– or technical centre as these places tend to be called now – is light, airy, clinical. Standards of appearance must match standards of production: no gaudy posters, no trainers. More than 190 people work here, designing and producing the cars, running the operation, marketing the commodity.

In a reception room, Flavio is joined by his 'inner cabinet' – Tom Walkinshaw, Ross Brawn and Rory Byrne. The mood is buoyant. The start of the season is little more than a month away. 'Taking on more technology means we may have reliability problems for the first quarter of the season, but after that I would expect us to get stronger,' says Tom in a quiet Scottish lilt which belies his solid frame and his even more solid resolve. He took Jaguar back to the top in sports cars and seeks similar success in Formula One.

Politics are in the air again, or, to be more accurate, on the ground, at Heathrow the following day. FISA's Formula One Commission decides to support the moves outlined by Briatore to cut costs this year and outlaw 'artificial driver aids' in 1994. There are controls on fuel and long-term plans to introduce oval racing. This represents the biggest shake-up for years. Williams and McLaren do not welcome the changes.

Patience is a virtue at testing

Williams are, however, in the Championship but Prost's future remains uncertain. The FISA President, Max Mosley, is unhappy about comments attributed to the Frenchman in a magazine article. His case will go before the World Council on 18 March. He will be granted a super licence for the opening race, in South Africa, four days later, but must then sweat it out.

This is Formula One, flexing its muscles for another season.

■ ■ ■

Benetton call off their scheduled trip to Estoril the following week at the eleventh hour and are back at Silverstone instead, grappling with a few gremlins. Patrese is still glum.

Another week on and another test at Silverstone. The morning is bright and sunny, though the chill wind could cut you in two. But then it always seems cold at this old airfield, locked in the heart of the country. Schumacher and Patrese arrive together in a red Ford Sierra. With them is one of the team's new test drivers, the Scot, Allan McNish.

Schumacher makes for the motorhome, and breakfast. No need to send out to the canteen – Stuart and Diana Spires, the team's regular 'Mum and Dad', are back in attendance. Patrese quickly changes into his race-suit and goes to work. The Camel Benetton Ford carries, for the first time, the logo of a new fuel supplier and sponsor, Elf Minol.

Patrese returns to the pits, technicians converge, warmers go on the tyres. The mechanics look as though they could use them. Their ordeal is not helped by the smell of bacon wafting through the air. 'It's still better than being stuck in the factory,' says one. Of course.

Every now and then a group of mechanics will peep down the pit lane towards the McLaren Ford garage. This is the team within Benetton's sights and their new drivers, Michael Andretti and Mika Hakkinen, are having a difficult time with the all-new car. The Benetton boys can scarcely stifle the odd titter.

Schumacher appears in his yellow overalls but also a bomber jacket. And he is attacking a sandwich. It appears to be lunch-time. There are those who say the German will have Patrese for supper.

Patrese expresses no concern. 'It is going to be tough for me with Michael as my team-mate, I know. He is very strong, he is fast and committed. But last year I was with Nigel, so it is nothing new.'

A phlegmatic smile accompanies a gesture which can be interpreted as 'What am I supposed to do or say?' What he does say is: 'I always like a new challenge and I still have my enthusiasm. I was not happy last week because the car was not working well, but now it is much better. I feel I have tested properly for the first time today. The gearbox is really good and now we have the active also. Williams are still ahead, especially on a power circuit like this, but we are getting closer and everybody is working like hell, 24 hours a day. There is a big, big effort here.'

Schumacher, meanwhile, has removed his jacket and strategically positioned himself on a wheel of his strategically positioned car, in the pit lane. He is filming a German television commercial and Flavio is on hand to assist the direction. Several takes are required. 'It's good that you do not understand German,' Michael says after cursing his fluffed lines again.

The orange blur of Silverstone Sid, jumping from his van and marching towards the set, makes most of the gathering aware that it's time to go back to the day job. Does this German producer know what he's taking on here? The message gets through, camera and sound equipment are removed and testing resumes.

Schumacher, who has clocked 1 minute 21.9 – within a second of Hill's best time for Williams – manages just three laps today. He's straight into a rhythm, putting up competitive times. An engineer reports to base: 'That Schumacher, he's something else. Goes straight out, cold tyres, and does a 26, 25, 24.'

The first spots of rain appear and Schumacher rushes off. He is due at a sponsors' function that evening in Cologne.

■　■　■

1 March, Treviso, Northern Italy. The weather would have you believe it's Silverstone. The Formula One racing team's strategy for 1993 is to be revealed at

Test truck and wet tyres at the ready

Benetton's HQ. The traditional majesty of Villa Minelli, the seventeenth-century office and nerve centre of the Benetton empire, contrasts with the modern, Lego-like plant with psychedelic metal roof.

Tom Walkinshaw explains that the team will start the season with the B193A, which has active suspension and semi-automatic transmission. From the third or fourth race they will run the B193B, which has new bodywork, a new aerodynamic package and a new monocoque. Also coming on stream is anti-lock braking and Ford's electronic throttle control, which is effectively a traction control system. Mid-season, Cosworth are planning to introduce Ford's new engine. Benetton are Ford's 'factory' team.

Tom is bullish. 'I believe we can establish ourselves in the first two and have a chance of a real run at the World Championship,' he says. 'It will be very close.' Flavio is similarly optimistic about the team's prospects of competing for the Championship.

Schumacher is more circumspect. 'It seems Riccardo and I have to go for it!' he says. 'I believe, as Tom says, we can win some races this year. As for winning the Championship, that is something else.'

Schumacher, Patrese and the three test drivers, McNish, Andrea Montermini and Paul Belmondo, pose for pictures while the caterers serve up pasta and risotto.

■　■　■

3 March, Silverstone. Ayrton Senna, still undecided as to whether he will compete this year, has his first winter test in the new McLaren. It is cold, he has a spin and says it is difficult to find a rhythm. But he is fast. The following day he is faster still. Faster, in fact, than anyone else here in the close season. His best time is 1 minute 20.27 – 0.8 of a second quicker than Hill, 1.7 seconds quicker than Schumacher.

Senna returns to Silverstone on Monday 8 March and announces he will race in South Africa the following Sunday. Hakkinen must watch.

CHAPTER 3

THE RACE IS ON

Winter wonderland has given way to a state of still greater confusion, especially in the Camel Benetton Ford camp. News of Senna's Silverstone times is reverberating through Formula One as the show rigs its tent at Kyalami for the opening round of the 1993 World Championship. It had seemed McLaren were in deep trouble. It certainly appeared Benetton had leapt ahead of them. Suddenly, the complexion of the contest has changed.

Gordon Message, frank as always, confesses: 'Yeah, they've surprised us. Even with Senna. It has to be a good car. We've got it to do, simple as that.'

Drivers and team personnel drift into South Africa over a period of several days. Coming out of a European winter to the heat and altitude of the Transvaal, accli-

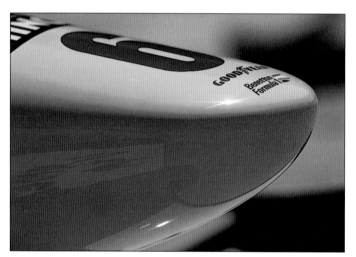

matisation is important. Some amuse themselves at Sun City, take in a leisurely safari, play golf or simply laze by the pool.

By the Thursday of race week all the set is more or less in place. Still the buzz surrounds McLaren. Michael Schumacher had always tempered his optimism and isn't likely to go overboard now. 'I just won't say stupid things,' he reasons. 'I will only be realistic and at the moment it is not realistic to talk about the Championship.'

Even though Benetton improved through the winter, Williams remained ahead, he points out. No matter what the margin was, they were still in front. Sure, he might get lucky, Williams could have a catalogue of catastrophes, but he was not going to expect that. And now Senna comes in with these times....

Schumacher talks down a good game and has been doing so since his extraordinary arrival in the late summer of 1991. One race weekend with Jordan was enough to convince Benetton he was worth poaching, whatever the controversial consequences, and sufficient to forewarn the driver of the expectations about to be draped over his shoulders. He was adamant he would not contemplate superstardom and be subjected to the 'intolerable pressures' which had burdened and buckled his compatriots Boris Becker and Steffi Graf.

Eighteen months on he has completed his first full season, won his first race and finished third in the Championship. There is no question about it, he is a star. Yet still he resists. 'I don't want to see all over the media that I am the next hero,' he says.

He has, in any case, apparently rendered himself immune to such a threat by rediscovering himself – and not reading the papers. 'Last year was a difficult year for me,' he says. 'So much happened so quickly and I took notice of what was being said in the newspapers, and on television. Now I don't read the papers. I believe only what I know to be true. This way there is not so much pressure. I don't feel it and I won't accept it. It is a question of attitude. Because of this attitude I am much more self-confident this year.

'Last year I was not so much myself as I am now. You have to come back to yourself. I have realised this. A little experience helps, of course, and I feel more mature. There is a German expression which, roughly translated, goes: "What you call in the wood comes back."'

Listening to Schumacher you cannot help but discern echoes of Senna, that other high-speed philosopher. It is suggested to Schumacher that his decision to find a pad in Monaco, along with Senna and the rest, is indicative of his desire to escape the pressures and hero-worshippers in his own land. 'It is also for the climate,' he maintains.

Michael Schumacher... one of the brightest talents for years

Schumacher had his skirmishes with Senna last season, makes no apologies for his aggression then and serves notice that he has no intention of becoming a shrinking violet this time. 'I try to race, to compete, to fight,' he says with a look of bewilderment that anyone should expect anything else. 'That is what we are here for and if that is a problem for some people they must learn to live with it.'

For all that, Michael contends the world of Formula One is not quite the jungle it is often portrayed as. 'It is not as cold as many people try to represent it. Sure, in the case of a couple of drivers it is not so good, but in general, the relationships between us are good. We are not all at war.'

He is appreciative of the home comforts he has at Benetton. 'Without this team I could not have had the success I have had already,' he stresses. 'It is not just the car. It is the people. They are just as important.

'When I was younger I had the right school at Mercedes. I made the correct decision to move from Jordan to Benetton. I had good advice, but the decision was mine. I have always made the right decision in my career, so I think I can say I am a lucky boy.'

There is, however, nothing lucky about Schumacher's performances on the track and he heads the new generation of drivers confronting the old order. A fresh season beckons, perhaps a different era, too.

'It is the natural way of things for new heroes to come through,' he acknowledges. 'Last year Alain Prost went away, this year Nigel Mansell has gone away. We still do not know whether Senna will have a full season. But there has to be change. If Damon Hill wins races, he will be the next hero for Britain.'

■   ■   ■

Riccardo Patrese... most experienced driver in the history of Formula One

A hot Friday morning greets the combatants for the first action of the 1993 Formula One season. Temperatures soar during the frenetic practice sessions, shortened by FISA to 45 minutes instead of an hour and a half in the morning, 45 minutes instead of an hour for the afternoon's qualifying.

Prost confirms the suspicions that he may have been 'sand-bagging' during the winter, holding something back. Not now. He is unleashing his Williams, and has to. Senna, in the McLaren, is demonstrating that his Silverstone test was no illusion. Benetton know the race is on, all right.

Schumacher takes up the challenge. He and his crew are still making adjustments, seeking the best chassis equation for this new Kyalami circuit. It is tighter than the old one, offering fewer opportunities for overtaking. Such, alas, is the trend with many of the modern tracks. Safety is, of course, a prime consideration. But that should not mean a sterile compromise. Barcelona has set the example for the rest. An advanced position on the grid would be welcomed here.

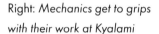

Right: *Mechanics get to grips with their work at Kyalami*

Below: *Tom Walkinshaw, Engineering Director*

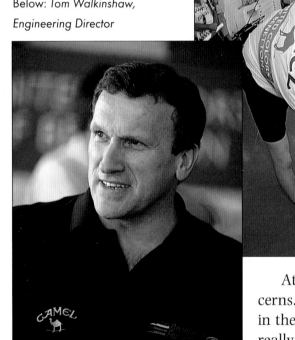

Facing page: *Storm brewing for Schumacher in the South African Grand Prix*

At the moment, the layout of the circuit is the least of Patrese's concerns. 'I think I'm suffering from not having done enough kilometres in the car. I'm still learning about it. Each lap it feels better, but I'm not really into it yet.'

Michael has a more productive morning, removes his helmet and balaclava, and nods his head in a manner which indicates: 'Not bad for starters'. He is third fastest in the session. Riccardo is 11th, 2.4 seconds slower than his young team-mate.

The debrief is an urgent crossfire of views and suggestions. This routine, digesting the times and information from the session and re-routing the strategy in terms of aerodynamics and settings, is enacted in every team up and down the pit lane. The findings govern changes to be made to the cars before qualifying, the actual scramble for grid positions. The cars run with a minimum requirement of fuel. The requirement now is sheer speed, not endurance.

Engineers and mechanics, given their instructions, set about the cars from front wing to rear. The activity is earnest and methodical. Each man has his job

and his responsibility. They now have more time between the sessions, but the shortened periods on the track mean greater pressure to get it right in the garage.

The two Benetton drivers knock chunks off their morning times as the cars screech through the first qualifying session. It is much the same story for the other teams. They have all made useful gains based on their work during the morning. Schumacher maintains his position – third – behind Prost and Senna, but in front of Hill, with a time of 1 minute 17.507 seconds. Patrese moves up to ninth on the provisional grid with 1 minute 19.341 seconds.

'I'm quite happy with the improvements we made to the car, although there are still a lot of things to do,' says Schumacher. 'We made some big changes between the two sessions and we even managed to improve the car further during qualifying. In fact, we wanted to make another change but there was simply not enough time. I had to go out on my second set and get on with it. There seemed to be a lot of traffic and I suppose that's the way it's going to be now that we have so little time.'

Patrese says: 'We worked on the balance and, on the first set of tyres this afternoon, it felt really good. On the second there was a lot of traffic, yellow flags, dirt on the track and so on. I think I could have gone half a second quicker. I hope I can go even better tomorrow.'

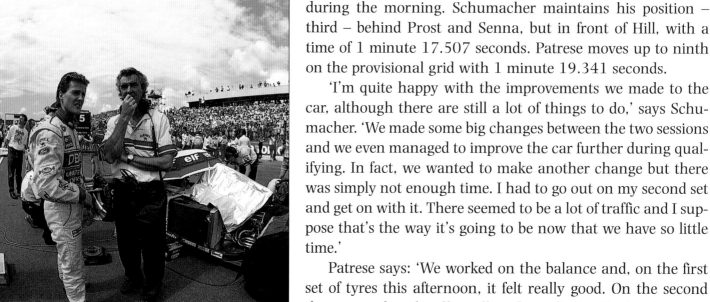

Pre-race tension... Michael Schumacher and Flavio Briatore on the grid at Kyalami

Complaints about the traffic are echoed by most of the drivers. Attempts to reduce costs have been generally well received, but the feeling is that the practice sessions have been made too short. Some suggest a compromise: longer sessions but a strict limit on the number of laps permitted each driver. The debate will go on.

So does the job in hand at Benetton. Tomorrow they have to make every minute of practice pay. In the morning the objective will be to get the optimum performance from the car in race trim, that is, prepared for the Grand Prix itself, with a full fuel load. In the afternoon the attention again switches to the contest for grid positions. For the mechanics work goes on deep into the evening, often into the night, sometimes through the night. It is a job for the enthusiast and more.

Saturday morning, and Schumacher is immersed in the task of finding the best race set-up. He is only 10th fastest in the unofficial session yet contends he is not dismayed. Patrese is third quickest, and distinctly happier. Schumacher reverts to qualifying mode in the afternoon and returns third place on the grid. His time: 1 minute 17.261 seconds. Patrese is seventh: 1 minute 18.676 seconds.

'I'm not sure if the circuit was quicker or not today, but we are still third on the grid,' says Michael. 'We have improved the car even further, but not as much as we wanted. The car was good on full tanks this morning and I'm looking forward to what promises to be an exciting race.'

Riccardo says: 'The car is not perfect yet but we are better than yesterday. I feel more comfortable with the car as I get more used to it. Overall, everything works well. I think I will have learned a lot more by the end of the 72 laps tomorrow.'

They retire to join the debrief. The psychology of this business demands optimism, yet the anxiety in the camp is both discernible and understandable. Schumacher may be third, but he is a second and a half adrift of the front-row pair, Prost and Senna. This was not what the team had envisaged. Now it is vital to make full use of the final practice session, the half-hour warm-up on Sunday morning.

The order on Sunday morning is still Prost-Senna-Schumacher, but the times are closer. Schumacher is a fighter, too. We may be in for a good race. There is another potentially critical consideration: the weather. It is still hot, but as we approach the start of the South African Grand Prix, dark clouds are gathering in the distance. If the rain arrives before the end, anything could happen. Prost admits he detests the wet, while Senna and Schumacher excel regardless. It is

Into combat... Riccardo Patrese pulls out of the Benetton garage

Prost's first race on this Kyalami track, as it is Hill's. Perhaps there is just that little more tension in the Williams camp.

Whatever is going through Prost's mind, he fluffs his start ('a problem with the clutch'). Through the first corner it's Senna-Hill-Prost-Schumacher. Then Hill, his inexperience exposed, spins and almost collects Prost. Schumacher slips into second place. Patrese is ninth. After a dozen laps the Italian, settling into his stride, is up to seventh. Michael, however, can hold Prost no longer and drops to third. 'I could see he was too quick, especially on the straights. I let him pass.'

Prost takes Senna on lap 24 and soon Schumacher is bustling by the Brazilian. The Benetton dives into the pits for fresh rubber just ahead of the McLaren but emerges from the pits just behind. Prost stops a lap later and retains the lead. Fears about excessive wear of the narrower tyres appear unfounded. One change should do. As the leading three emphasise their dominance, Patrese's patience carries him up to fourth place.

Michael is hounding the McLaren, eager for an opening, a slight lapse in concentration, a momentary loss of momentum. He feels he has a chance on lap 40 and darts for the inside at a right-hander. Senna refuses to give way, they touch wheels and the Benetton spins out of the race. 'I felt I was slightly quicker than Senna but it was difficult to find a way past,' says Schumacher. 'I did feel I had the right opportunity to make a move at that time.'

Others in the camp doubt the wisdom of the attack. Just there? With Senna? Was it worth the risk with 32 laps left? In a cockpit, however, you have to make a judgment and go with it. That is racing. Schumacher, lest we forget, is still a relative novice. He is learning and that experience is doubtless stored away. It will not be wasted.

Riccardo, meanwhile, is up to third. Only until lap 47. He spins and, despite his frantic efforts to recover, the Benetton beds itself in the gravel trap. Worse still, he climbs out and the marshals, in their desperate endeavours to pull the car back, contrive to haul it into its driver. 'A front wheel bruised my right leg quite a bit,' says Riccardo.

It has been a bruising race all round for Camel Benetton Ford. As Prost, Senna and Mark Blundell, of Ligier Renault, emerge from the late deluge unscathed and mount the podium, the team who scored points in every race of 1992 begin the inquests on a blank start to 1993. Schumacher is urging the introduction of traction control as soon as possible. Senna's pace out of the corners illustrated the value of the device, he observes. The team hear him but they don't want to be panicked into using traction control before it is ready.

Talking tactics... Michael Schumacher and Ross Brawn

What is clear is that all the team are keen to get the new car, the B193B, into action. They will test it before the next race, in Brazil, on 28 March, and perhaps press it into service for the following round of the Championship, the Easter Sunday running of the Grand Prix of Europe, at Donington Park.

■ ■ ■

Schumacher joins the important Silverstone test. This opening phase of the season, with races in South Africa and South America, is demanding on all concerned, but Michael is anxious to hasten the debut of the B193B. He is quickly about his business. Nothing particularly unusual about that, perhaps. But this is a new car, and new cars tend to need nursing through their first paces. Schumacher, however, is soon reducing the lap times to competitive figures.

After just three laps of the South Circuit the car is half a second faster than the old one. Schumacher sustains the rate of improvement on the second day. Now he is hacking a full second off the B193A's time. Schumacher and the Benetton crew are humming.

Anxious wait for Patrese as the crew work on his car

'It feels incredibly quick,' enthuses Michael. 'It is quicker in slow and quick corners, and has much less drag. I know we have taken a big step forward. It's very exciting. The new car gives us an all-round performance improvement. I must say I would like to take it to Sao Paulo.' That is not possible, but the fresh injection of optimism should serve Schumacher and the team well at Interlagos, scene of the Brazilian Grand Prix.

For that race meeting, FISA decides, practice and qualifying sessions will revert to durations of one and a half hours and one hour respectively. Each day, however, cars will be limited to 23 laps in the morning and 12 in the afternoon. Teams will have 28 tyres per weekend, plus an 'evaluation' set. This extra set may not be used in qualifying.

FISA also announces, after a farcical 'hearing' in Paris, that Alain Prost will not be suspended for his alleged criticism of the sport's governing body. The Williams driver says he is 'sorry' and that, it appears, is the end of that.

Formula One is congratulating itself on the South African Grand Prix, conscious that the 'show' took a bit of a pounding from the public and the pundits last year. Okay, so Alain Prost's Williams Renault was well clear at the end, and there were only five finishers, but hadn't it been a splendid scrap between Ayrton Senna's McLaren Ford and Michael Schumacher's Camel Benetton Ford? What's more, Mark Blundell had brought through his Ligier Renault in third place, the new Sauber team had showed up well and there were Minardi in the points. Lotus are bound to get stronger and Footwork have a new car coming up.

Let's go

Surely we are in for a competitive, entertaining season.

The propaganda machinery is at work in response to the challenge from the IndyCar series, which now has Nigel Mansell, Formula One's reigning world champion, topping its bill. Mansell wins his opening race, a thrilling street fight at Surfers' Paradise, Australia, and the media appraisal, especially in Britain, is effusive.

The IndyCar race is the subject of much gossip along the pit lane on the Thursday at Interlagos. Prost says he watched it but was not overly impressed. Besides, he argues, after the first three the rest were nowhere. It is completely different from Formula One and of no threat or relevance to Grand Prix racing. Sure, he had been a comfortable winner in the end at Kyalami, but McLaren had problems and Benetton have their new car coming along.

Benetton's new car is also a subject of much gossip. Is it as good as the grapevine is suggesting? Schumacher says he believes so. When will it be raced? Donington, that's the plan. This, though, is Brazil and Benetton prefer to quell the talk about the new car. They have to get on with the job here using the old one. It could be a tough weekend. This is more of a power circuit than Kyalami, with a steep gradient towards the final corner. Williams have the benefit of a V10 engine. There's no question that the Didcot operation ought to be at the front of the grid for this one.

Events on Friday reinforce that opinion. Williams set the pace from the start. The weather – hot, with an ever-present threat from grey clouds – is symbolically oppressive for the rest. The temperature is certainly rising in the Benetton pit. Patrese is animated. He cannot find the grip he requires. His exasperation is evident in his gestures. At the end of free practice he is 11th. After the first qualifying session he is down to 13th.

Schumacher is a little more content, yet far from satisfied. He is seventh in the morning, fourth in the afternoon, behind Prost, Hill and Senna, who has agreed to compete in another race, his home race, but still refuses to commit himself for the full season. Michael says: 'There is a big gap between Williams and everybody else but I think a lot of that comes from the advantage they have on this particular circuit. It's quite different to Kyalami – not so flat and very bumpy in places.'

The gap and the problems occupy the drivers' minds all evening. They are among the Elf squad of drivers who make it to the fuel company's annual party at a luxurious house in a Sao Paulo suburb, in spite of the fumbling efforts of police out-riders, Brazil's answer to the Keystone Cops. Sombre reality is soon taking over from the light relief. Patrese stands alone, pushing slices of fruit around his plate. He and Schumacher return to their hotel still mentally wrestling with their work.

Saturday morning and early clear blue skies quickly give way to a gloomy cloud cover. More symbolism? Schumacher feels he may see a ray of hope. He conveys his thoughts to his team; changes are accordingly made. He is fifth in the unofficial session but undeterred. Nor does a spin, in qualifying, distract him from his course. He goes third, only for Senna to come back at him. Fourth it is.

The modern tools of the trade

Patrese also begins to make significant progress. He is ninth in the morning and up to sixth on the starting grid.

Schumacher says: 'I often find I cannot sleep because my mind is running over the problems with the car. I was like that last night. But I came in this morning with a new plan and it worked for both of us. We improved quite a bit. The work is with you all the time.'

Patrese says: 'At least I feel now that I am in a position to finish comfortably in the points. The trouble is that the effort spent working on the qualifying set-up today meant I was unable to try running with full tanks. There is a long way to go yet, but at least this is an improvement.'

Michael is less pleased to learn that he has come in for some criticism in a German publication. Fourth, it seems, is unacceptable back home. 'What do they expect?' he asks, visibly irritated. 'Do they want me to be champion in my second year?'

■ ■ ■

Sunday 28 March. Race day, 6.57 a.m. Riccardo Patrese appears in the lobby of the five-star Trans-America Hotel. He shuffles along the marble floor, by the palms, towards the doors. He looks pensive, perhaps apprehensive. He checks his watch.

It's 7.02 when his eye is caught by the big, bustling frame of Flavio Briatore. They exchange light-hearted banter about their arrangements to meet and leave for the circuit at seven o'clock, and disappear through the swing doors together.

Outside, the day is alight. Gentle sunshine casts a sympathetic glow on the less opulent quarters of this sprawling city. Here, as anywhere else in the Third World, you are constantly in conflict with your conscience. The admission price for today's race is more than the average monthly wage in Sao Paulo.

Nothing is spared for the stars of this show. The police out-riders are back, filing past the front of the hotel in readiness for their next assignment. Drivers and team personnel have now gathered in numbers, waiting for their cars to be brought to them. A tiny, mop-haired figure in shorts, jaunty, smiling, joins the milling throng. By his side is a large man in green blazer and tie. It is considered prudent to give Alain Prost a minder in Ayrton Senna's country. A step behind is Prost's track-suited physiotherapist. A cumbersome saloon rolls up; Prost takes the wheel and drives off with his police escort. The security guards patrolling the roof of the hotel can relax.

■　■　■

Little more than ten minutes away, a queue of humanity wraps itself around the perimeter wall of the Interlagos circuit, patiently inching towards the gate. These people know the odds are with Prost and Williams, yet they yearn for it to be Senna's day. If Christian Fittipaldi and Rubens Barrichello, the other Brazilian drivers, do well, so much the better.

It is just after eight o'clock and all is calm in garage 7. Three Camel Benetton Fords, their wheels removed, sit in silent anticipation, pointing out to the filling main stand. It is both normal and practical for teams to have the two race cars at either side of the garage, with the spare car in the middle. All three cars should be thoroughly prepared for the warm-up session and, this afternoon, the Grand Prix itself.

Engineers and mechanics painstakingly tend the B193As. One squats, punching at a computer. Others bend over the docile beasts, probing, prodding, adjusting, like surgeons at work on a patient in the operating theatre.

At 8.18 the drivers emerge from their enclave, a partitioned area at the back of the garage. In Europe the teams have their own motorhomes, complete with just about every imaginable comfort. Here, they must make do with more modest facilities. Michael Schumacher strides purposefully to the front of the garage and has a word in the ear of Frank Dernie, an experienced engineer and aerodynamicist who joined Benetton from Ligier. Before that he worked for Williams and Lotus. Photographers focus on the slim German. He looks confident, self-assured. He usually does. Some say he is arrogant. This is not a game for the timid.

Patrese stalks, hands on hips. A familiar pose. He pauses for brief consultation with an engineer and stalks again. His expression, serious though not stern, never changes. This is a man about to go to work.

Ross Brawn surveys the scene from the front of the garage. He has cans on his ears, radios at his hips, clipboard in his embrace. He could be a film director. One man conspicuous by his absence is Tom Walkinshaw. He is back at base, overseeing work on the new car.

Schumacher runs into the back of the garage, leaving the photographers peering over their lenses in bewilderment. 'I think that's nature calling,' says a PR lady, softly. He returns, pulls on his balaclava, helmet and gloves, and climbs into the middle car. Now there is even more attention on the young star. At 8.25, five minutes

Above: *Eye of the Tiger called Schumacher*

Left: *Schumacher takes his seat for the Brazilian Grand Prix*

before the start of warm-up, Schumacher gives the signal for the car to be fired up and he steers his way to the end of the pit lane, followed by a posse of mechanics, who must start him up again when the track is opened.

Activity around Patrese is more sedate. He has never been one to sit around at the end of the pit lane, just to be out on the track a few seconds ahead of the rest. Briatore, donning his cans, strides through the garage, across the pit lane and takes up his position on the pit wall. At 8.29 Patrese's car comes to life and he slides into the line of cars.

The green light unleashes 25 Grand Prix cars for the last half-hour of practice. Ivan Capelli, in the Jordan Hart, has failed to qualify. He will part company with the team before the next race. This session is directed solely towards the Grand Prix. It does not affect grid positions. Cars are in race trim, the fuel tanks full. Drivers and teams will clutch at any final scrap of information which can be gleaned from these few laps.

Schumacher returns to the pits after just one lap and is pushed back into the garage. He has given the spare car a systems and handling check, in case it should be needed by either driver, and now climbs from that to his race car. Patrese is back ... Schumacher is out again ... Schumacher is back ... Patrese is out again. It is 8.36. The mood and tempo in garage 7 have changed dramatically since half an

More checks for Schumacher's car at Interlagos

hour ago. Now the activity is intense. For all the banks of computers and telemetry equipment, there's still a place for a man with a screwdriver. It's quite comforting.

Michael sits patiently in his car as his crew go to work again. Warmers are on the tyres. He peers at the lap times appearing on a small monitor placed in front of him. Off come the tyre warmers, away goes the monitor and out, again, goes Schumacher. A mechanic applies a quick polish to the spare car. Not a second is wasted.

Nine figures line Benetton's stretch of the pit wall, logging times and manning the boards which pass on the information to the drivers as they flash by. The pit board is still a vital piece of equipment. That, too, is quite comforting. Half a dozen Benetton mechanics have to skip smartly as Jean Alesi's Ferrari booms into the adjoining pit. Benetton have a 30-strong team in evidence here, plus three press, PR and marketing women. Stuart and Diana Spires are out at the back, preparing lunch for the team and guests.

It's still only 8.45 as Schumacher is wheeled into the pits yet again. He is talking, via the radio link, to his engineers. Occasionally he nods his head. Now he gives a thumbs-up sign. All, apparently, is under control. The tyre warmers are on again as adjustments are made to the front and rear wings. Yellow chalk is being scrawled on the front left tyre, the pressure and temperature already noted. It is a conveyor belt of routine little jobs.

The Ford Cosworth behind Schumacher growls into action once more. It's 8.49. Eleven minutes of the session remain. A couple of engineers share a joke. The mood is good. Schumacher's pit board shows P3 – 21.7 (currently third fastest in the session with a time of 1 minute 21.7 seconds). Patrese is P8 – 22.6.

Patrese returns to the pits at 8.51. His gestures are more agitated than those of his partner. A flurry of work around his car and, at 8.53, he is off again.

Schumacher is P4. Alesi's car catches the attention of the Benetton boys again. It is smoking. The clock shows 8.58. Schumacher is P5, Patrese P4. Two mechanics follow the progress of a statuesque lady in figure-hugging attire, who just happens to be passing by.

At precisely nine o'clock, Schumacher comes in. His pit board indicates P6. A minute later Patrese is in. He has P5. Ahead of them are: Prost, Hill, Senna and Wendlinger.

Michael jumps from his car and briskly makes for the back. Riccardo is not in such a hurry. He seems happier. He talks to the engineers as the ritual industry around the cars commences. Off comes the bodywork, in go the heads and hands.

The engine boys fire up Schumacher's V8 for a quick check, then Patrese's. The Italian ambles into the back, rearranging his sweaty hair. This half-hour episode will be repeated on the morning of every race, ending four hours before the scheduled start of the race.

Suddenly the pace slackens, the tension lifts. Ahead is still a long day, and this is as much of a breather as the team will get. At least it seems they don't have an engine change on their hands. One mechanic takes the chance to light a cigarette.

The drivers have their own team's debriefing, then the regular official briefing by FISA officials to go through any particular points of procedure. Then they will have a little lunch and try to relax. At some circuits they may have to put in an appearance for sponsors and their guests.

Benetton's drivers are back in their lair; the team are working through the chores which accompany the countdown to the Grand Prix. Frank Dernie snatches the opportunity of a plate of pasta. He eats standing up. 'The trouble is, there is never enough time between the sessions to get the work done,' he says. 'There is so much work to be done overnight, too. These days there is more and more work for the engineers because of the active suspension and so on.'

If FISA stand by their proposals for 1994, the onus will revert to the mechanics. Active suspension and other such aides are due to be outlawed.

The track opens to the Formula One cars again at 12.30 for the one o'clock race. As the cars make their way around the circuit, stop for that final check and slot into place on the grid, team officials look anxiously skywards. The afternoon is overcast and the chances are we're going to have showers or even a deluge.

Prost has a clean start this time but Hill leaves an opening and Senna goes through. Andretti and Berger make a spectacular first-corner exit. Schumacher soon shakes off Alesi for fourth place and settles in with the chasing pack. Patrese, however, is having problems after completing two laps and can only coast to retirement. His active suspension oil cooler has split and he is losing hydraulic fluid. 'Nothing would work, and there was nothing anyone could do,' he says, turning away in anguish.

It seems there is nothing anyone can do about Prost. Surely he is heading for his second win. Hill takes Senna for second place. It is looking good for Williams. A stop-and-go penalty for Senna eases Schumacher up to third. Twenty-five laps into the race there's a rustling in the stands along the pit straight. Out comes the rainwear, up go the umbrellas. The first spots become a light mist, then a steady drizzle, then a downpour.

The leading drivers make for the pits and wet tyres. All, that is, except Prost. Schumacher's stop is anything but routine. The car falls off the jack and mechanics have to lift it to make the tyre change. Then there's a problem with the wheel nut on the front right.

Inexplicably, Prost continues. He completes 29 laps and still goes on. The straight is awash and strewn with debris from crashed cars. Prost is into a slide,

Facing page: Patrese's Brazilian Grand Prix is short-lived

helpless as his Williams clips Fittipaldi's stricken Minardi and is dumped into the gravel trap. The locals are jubilant.

The pace car – or safety car as Formula One prefers to call it – appears for the first time since the system was sanctioned in July 1992, and holds the cars in an orderly line while the track is cleared. Its job done, and done well, it peels away. Hill leads, from Senna and Schumacher.

Dry patches show up on the track as the rain relents and Senna and Schumacher sense the moment to revert to slicks. Schumacher's planned charge is stifled. He has also incurred a stop-and-go penalty, for overtaking Luca Badoer under yellow flags. He gingerly picks his way through a still wet and congested pit lane. He is down to ninth and only 29 laps remain. He feels a podium place is out of reach. Senna, meanwhile, is into the lead.

Still, Michael gives it a go. And how. With 15 laps left he is up to fifth. He is chasing Blundell. With six to go, the No. 5 Benetton is through to fourth. Now Schumacher is hounding Johnny Herbert's Lotus Ford. He attacks and goes ahead, only for Herbert to sneak back on the inside. Three laps from the end of a momentous race, Michael strikes again and this time the Englishman has no response. Interlagos celebrates a superb victory by Senna, but Schumacher has produced a similarly outstanding performance to take third place behind Hill's Williams.

'A brilliant result for us,' enthuses Michael. 'It was like a

Celebration for Schumacher after a brilliant drive to third place at Interlagos

victory for us after all the problems we had. I had endless worries today, so to come out of it on the podium is unbelievable.'

■   ■   ■

Late that evening, the executive lounge at Sao Paulo's international airport might be the pit lane back at Interlagos. There is Alesi ... at the other side Alboreto ... over here Brundle and Blundell ... and now enters Prost.

Schumacher is perched near the door with his manager, Willi Weber, sipping a soft drink. He is relaxed, contented. He knows he has driven brilliantly. His attention is caught by the small fair-haired figure swaggering into the lounge. Herbert does a double take. 'You —,' exclaims Herbert, glaring at the German. Herbert holds his expression for a few frozen moments, then he, and Schumacher, explode into laughter. They shake hands and exchange congratulations.

'We gave them a good race, though, didn't we?' says Herbert. 'I enjoyed that. Well done.'

Schumacher is bubbling. 'At the end I had no gears, no oil, no water,' he says, counting the ailments on his fingers. 'The car was completely gone,' he summarises with a dismissive wave of the hand. 'I nearly lost it. Did you see? I was very happy to make it.'

Michael's flight is called. More handshakes and he makes for the gate, leaving Flavio to express Benetton's frustrations. He rolls his head from side to side, the way Italians do to convey mixed emotions. 'Yes, it is a great drive by Michael and we have a good result, but it could have been a win,' he contends, now sitting on the table cleared of Schumacher's glass.

He argues that Schumacher's stop-and-go penalty was harsh and that it cost his protégé the chance to catch Hill and Senna. Schumacher had, after all, been the fastest man on the circuit at the end.

'Look,' says Briatore, painting the scene with his hands. 'Michael is behind Badoer. Badoer brakes, moves over. Michael just keeps going. Okay, so Senna also had a stop-and-go penalty. But he had a dry pit lane. We had a wet pit lane, cars in the way. We lost a minute, maybe more. We could now have a win,' he concludes, slapping his lap.

There is, however, ample consolation for Benetton and Formula One, as Briatore, a shrewd businessman, appreciates. 'It was good for television, heh? A beautiful race.'

A great show indeed....

CHAPTER 5

THE NEW BABY

The ten days between the Brazilian Grand Prix and the start of proceedings at Donington are among the most important in Camel Benetton Ford's season. All the teams are collating the information so far, taking stock, reappraising. Despite the altitude and abnormal circumstances of the first two races, they will have a reasonable indication of their own state of health compared with their opponents'. Some may be reassured they are on the right path, others may feel a slight shift in course is required, others still that they might as well go back to base and start all over again. Benetton have already decided to push ahead with their new car. It will be put through more testing at Silverstone and then pressed into service at the Grand Prix of Europe.

Riccardo Patrese is on duty at Silverstone's South circuit. He covers 40 laps on an unsettled first day, 100 on a better second. The B193B looks very much like the B193A, retaining the distinctive shark-like nose. However, Ross Brawn explains: 'It is virtually a completely new car. Last year's was a passive car in which we were able to fit active. This has been conceived as an active car and to accommodate the new tyres. It is lighter and the aerodynamic package is new, so although it may appear outwardly the same it is quite a lot different.'

A frenetic day for all concerned at Donington Park

Into another race week but still there is more testing to be done. Now Michael Schumacher is at Silverstone with the B193B. The stint completed, it really is time to christen the new baby.

■ ■ ■

Donington Park is a piece of rolling English countryside just beyond the runway of East Midlands Airport. They held Grands Prix here in the 1930s. Those marvellous Auto Unions and Mercedes Benz were brought over for the 1937 and 1938 races and held the crowds spellbound. So did the driving skills of Rosemeyer and Nuvolari. No one was more engrossed than a youngster called Tom Wheatcroft, who cycled the 30 miles from his home and paid half a crown to watch the great international stars of the day. In the 1970s that same Tom Wheatcroft, by then a successful builder, bought the old circuit, created his racing museum and launched his campaign to put cars back on the track. Once he had won his battle to revive Donington Park, he set his sights on bringing to life his boyhood fantasies and hosting his own Formula One World Championship Grand Prix.

He confronted stern resistance and prejudice, yet defied the sceptics by turning the British motorcycling Grand Prix into a profit-making exercise and felt his circuit was worthy of Formula One. On a number of occasions he seemed close, on a number of occasions he was disappointed. Then, in the autumn of 1992, the Asian Grand Prix, due to be held at the Japanese circuit of Autopolis, was dropped from the 1993 calendar for financial reasons. Throughout the guessing game which followed, there was no suggestion that Donington might fill the gap, but FISA announced that 70-year-old Wheatcroft was to realise his dream. He would stage the Grand Prix of Europe on 11 April, Easter Day.

Wheatcroft was in Australia when he heard the news. 'For about twenty minutes the feeling was wonderful,' he said. 'I felt like a million dollars. I'd wanted this as much as anything in life. But then I began to get a strange feeling about it all. I suddenly started to wonder if anything would go wrong and take it away from us again. Well, I'd been promised a race five times and we'd be the only privately owned circuit to have a Championship event. I couldn't help having my doubts.'

Those doubts were unfounded, though there remained many who questioned the wisdom of taking Formula One to Donington. Alain Prost was chief among those who considered the track unsuitable. He thought it was too tight and dangerous. He said it would be like driving around his kitchen. Other drivers also had their fears on grounds of safety. Wheatcroft and FISA addressed those fears, and over the winter months £600,000 was spent on improvements, most of that on safety measures. Eighty thousand tons of gravel was brought in for the run-off areas. Additional grandstand seating was ordered. Circuit officials were preparing for – and hoping for – a crowd of 80,000-plus.

■　■　■

It is the Thursday of race week and England feels as if it is still in the grip of winter. The transporters and motorhomes are in place and the first rumbles of engines can be heard from the row of garages. They are rather less spacious than those now demanded, and regarded as standard, by Formula One. But then there is much about Donington Park which does not look or feel like Formula One. There is a low-key, quaint feel to it. More like a club meeting than a World Championship Grand Prix and, in a sense, all the more endearing for it.

Since this is a new Formula One circuit, there is to be an hour's 'testing practice' this afternoon. For all the teams it represents a vital opportunity to familiarise themselves with the track and gain guidelines to the required car settings. The Benetton camp are particularly anxious to make full use of the extra session. They are still familiarising themselves with the B193B.

A grey, scowling sky spits raindrops as the engineers and mechanics prepare the cars for Michael Schumacher and Riccardo Patrese. They would appreciate all the dry running they can get, but the signs are they may not be so lucky. Well, this is Easter in England!

A spiteful drizzle plays its tricks as the 26 drivers – including Jordan's replacement for Ivan Capelli, the experienced Belgian, Thierry Boutsen – pick their way around the two-and-a-half-mile circuit. Several drivers have spins and the session ends with a slightly unusual mixture of names behind the Williams Renaults of Prost and Damon Hill: Gerhard Berger's Ferrari, Ayrton Senna's McLaren, Johnny Herbert's Lotus, Martin Brundle's Ligier, Philippe Alliot's Larrousse and J. J. Lehto's Sauber.

Schumacher's Benetton, restricted by a split oil cooler, is next, a modest ninth. Patrese's Benetton is 12th. These have been unsteady first steps for the new baby, but the weather has not helped and you can reach out and touch the frustration inside the camp.

Michael is as much confused as disappointed. Certainly some of the enthusiasm of a fortnight ago has been diluted. He is guarded. 'Unfortunately, today I was not able to do as many laps as I wanted. But I believe the car will be really good for the weekend. How good, I can't say.' How about the circuit? 'The only feeling I've got is that it is quite narrow, tight, and really difficult to overtake. I need to do more laps to know about the safety.'

Patrese takes the safe route to score two points in the Grand Prix of Europe

Riccardo says he is 'very positive' about the new car. 'It is definitely quicker than the old one. Today I was learning the circuit. Tomorrow I can say more about its potential. If the weather is unstable it is a gamble for everybody. I prefer it to be dry.'

Another complication is clouding Benetton's horizon. Senna and McLaren, having won in Brazil, are lobbying hard for engine parity with Ford's 'factory' team. Senna says he is led to believe the latest spec engine, available by contractual right only to Benetton, produces at least 20 bhp more than the customer powerplant supplied to McLaren. (Lotus and Minardi are the other customer teams.) Tom Walkinshaw denies such a claim. He insists Benetton's advantage is a mere eight bhp. But he is equally adamant the deal is cast in stone, and stresses that his team are guaranteed more advanced units than those supplied to the rest.

There is, though, clearly a dilemma for Benetton. Do they remain entrenched and risk antagonising Ford, and perhaps jeopardise their long-term relationship? And if there is so little power differential between the

Rain men... Frank Dernie and Michael Schumacher

engines, would it not be better to take off the gloves and square up to McLaren in hand-to-hand combat? The internal debate will doubtless go on.

Friday brings no meteorological or political respite. The day is wet and eventful, with more than a dozen cars having spins worthy of the term. Schumacher is second, behind Senna, in the morning. Patrese is 11th. In qualifying, Michael's car joins the casualty list. He is on the power a little too early coming out of Melbourne Hairpin, squirms into the wall and bends a wheel. 'It can happen; I was trying too much,' he confesses.

Schumacher runs back to the pits and Patrese knows he must condense his session and then hand over his car to his team-mate. The afternoon is becoming all too frenetic for the Italian, and a 'misunderstanding' with the pit crew compounds the anxiety. He climbs from his car, the despair etched in his face. His time will leave him 13th on the provisional grid. 'I wanted to stay out longer for just one run, but by the time we had

The Formula One World Championship comes to Donington Park

discussed this and I stayed out for another lap, I lost some momentum and the track was very busy,' says Riccardo. 'To have only 12 laps in the wet like this is ridiculous. It is so difficult to find a clear lap, away from the spray. You have to take risks on your last lap.'

The No. 6 Benetton becomes the No. 5 Benetton and Schumacher again ventures out into the rain. He manages seventh fastest time. He takes a philosophical line: 'Tomorrow is another day, thankfully, and it cannot be worse than this.'

Saturday is another day entirely. It is bright, sunny and dry, if still fresh. Gearbox and exhaust problems ensure Schumacher is not spoiled but he is fourth fastest in the morning. Patrese is toiling for the right set-up and is 12th. Both drivers make progress in qualifying, though Patrese is grounded by a gremlin in the

gearbox electronics. He has to accept 10th place on the grid.

Michael feels he is at last getting his teeth into the weekend. The front row is clearly the preserve of the Williams pair, Prost and Hill, but the real contest is for third place. Into the final five minutes, Schumacher edges clear of Senna with a 1 minute 12.2. Senna, in a typically late surge, responds to post a 12.1. Schumacher has one more chance, and conjures a 12.0. He will start the race from third place on the grid.

Now the smile is back. 'I have to be happy,' he says. 'Over the winter I was talking a lot about being in third position behind Williams. Unfortunately, we couldn't get there in the first two races because McLaren had done such a good job during the winter, which surprised us. But today I think we surprised everybody by coming here with a new car and very little experience with it. Today was the only day we could set up the car for the circuit and we improved a lot. The end result was exactly what we have been hoping to achieve, third place ahead of the McLarens. We started today with no knowledge and developed the car in 30 laps. We still don't have traction control and we especially miss that in the rain. Overall, I am encouraged. I hope we have a dry race because I know how difficult it can be here in the wet.'

He must have feared he was tempting fate. The scene on Sunday morning is wet, cool and frankly depressing. Those long queues so detested at Silverstone suddenly seem like home. Can this really be a Grand Prix? You feel for Tom Wheatcroft. The drivers and teams are feeling for themselves. They are back to the lottery. The breakfast-time drizzle becomes a steady downpour as warm-up approaches. As for race time, the forecasters suggest there could be brighter periods. Then more rain.

Most people in this game will say they can cope with wet or dry conditions. What they do not like is something in between. The only safe route then is to compromise with set-up and driving technique, but that can be unsatisfactory and unsuccessful. It is a day for quick reflexes in and out of the cockpit.

Schumacher, wearing a bright green cap and a dark jacket over his yellow race-suit, appears in the Camel Benetton Ford compound on a mountain bike. He seems cheerful still. He had a good day in the dry but he is one of the better drivers in the wet and the rain will not be appreciated in the Williams camp. The race could be wide open. He sprints from the garage to the truck to dump his jacket and sprints back again. Patrese is more languid. He still seems less than cheerful.

At 9.25 Schumacher dries the soles of his shoes with a vigorous rub and climbs into his car. (This race starts at the more regular time of 2.00 p.m. so warm-up is 9.30 to 10.00.) He and the others are not in a rush to get to the end of the pit lane today. No one wants to sit in the rain. His car is fired up at precisely 9.30, Patrese's at 9.33.

The shuttle routine is under way. Patrese is running the spare today and steam rises from the treaded Goodyears as he is brought in to change cars. He has a spin but returns in one piece. Conditions are now appalling. Passing cars trail spectacular plumes of spray and sparks.

Life is no easier for the pit crew. They are wearing their yellow and blue wet-suits but the rain seeps everywhere and numbs the hands. Normal warning noises can be lost in the wash and confusion of a day like this, so the senses of team personnel have to be extra sharp. Today, this is an even more dangerous environment. Those on the pit wall who can, huddle under the small Benetton awning. So this is wetting the baby's head!

Patrese is back out on the circuit and engineers examine the car he has left behind. Ross Brawn, a large, bespectacled, studious man, joins the investigation, calmly issues instructions and his men nod acknowledgement. In a corner of the garage, Ford Cosworth engineers digest the telemetry information.

At the end of the session, Schumacher's pit board shows P6. Patrese is P23. Another job has still to be tackled. 'Pit-stop practice coming up, pit-stop practice coming up,' is the radio message from Frank Dernie, Schumacher's race engineer. The crew had problems in Brazil and may be busy this afternoon. Michael steers into the required spot; the change is swift and clean.

Some ten minutes after the session, as after all sessions, the drivers and a group of engineers, led by Brawn, assemble in the inner sanctum of the transporter for a debrief. This is a secretive, almost mystical ritual, the discussions and findings closely guarded. The debrief area is a raised section at the front of the truck. Eleven men slide along the bench seats either side of a two-tier table, which is covered with papers. A couple of cans and plastic cups have been placed on the top tier. Brawn settles and pores over the official time sheets, which provide a breakdown of every lap by every driver in the session just completed.

Given the very strong prospect of tyre changes during the race, driver-to-team radio communications are going to be of crucial importance. Dernie says: 'If

Michael tells you he's coming into the pits, we've got plenty of time to get the tyres ready. I can hear him clear as a bell. Brilliant.'

Fuel consumption can also be affected by the conditions, and appropriate contingency plans are considered with the two engine men in Ford jackets. The situation will be under constant scrutiny right up to race time.

The drivers are taken through an engine check list. 'Cut-out, noises, vibration?' Schumacher and Patrese, sitting opposite each other, report no such problems and express their satisfaction. The engine men, looking suitably content, collect their papers and depart.

This debrief, like most of the debriefs, goes on for about 25 minutes. Brawn and his colleagues delve deep into technical areas, communicating in mind-blowing jargon. On the best of days, this part of the business is an exact science. Car settings measured in millimetres can decide a driver's fate. On this day the race set-up and strategy have to be influenced by the uncertainty of the elements. The teams will have to be in a position to react to changes as late as possible.

An hour before the start of the race, the rain has stopped and the scene appears to be brightening. It is an illusion. The rain will come and go all day and the drivers and teams are in for one of their most difficult races of this or any season.

Those lining up on the grid have wet tyres, but J. J. Lehto is gambling. He has to switch to the spare car and start from the pit lane, so he feels he may as well go with slicks. The scramble for the first corner, Redgate, is less eventful than many suspected, the Williams pair leading the way through, followed by Wendlinger's Sauber. Schumacher, conscious of Senna's threat, momentarily has the Brazilian covered, but the McLaren takes him out of the corner. By the end of the first lap Senna is in the lead and Michael knows he has a mighty task on his hands. Through the opening stages he holds sixth place, while Patrese runs ninth.

Soon positions and fortunes change as rapidly as the tyres. Some come in too early, and pay the price. Others stay out too long, and lose their way. Just when it seems slicks are the order of the rest of the day, the drizzle returns to give the drama another fiendish twist. It may, though, be just a brief shower. It may be prudent – if temporarily precarious – to stay out and be one step ahead of the pack should the track begin to dry again.

The thoughts and permutations are spinning through the heads of the drivers. Michael is on slicks, negotiating the 23rd lap, when he spins out of the race. 'I was shifting down to third gear and my rear wheels locked,' he says. 'I was pushing hard and on the limit. I just lost the car and that was it. The end. I'm very disappointed with this weekend. I am sure the team feel let down. All I can say is "sorry" and I'll try and make up for it next time.'

Schumacher's comments are refreshingly apologetic and considerate. The boys in any team can put up with most things, but they don't like to be taken for granted. This has been a long, testing weekend for everyone. Here they are, in the rain, and one of their cars has been thrown off. The last thing they want to hear is a driver feeling sorry for himself.

*Respite at last for Patrese at
Donington Park*

A lap after his partner's demise, Patrese is in the pits for a change to wets. Mindful of his fruitless first two outings this year, he is intent on finishing. He abandons all notions of going for glory. His concern is to go the distance, secure in the knowledge that that will earn him and his team some points. This conservative route involves two further pit stops and steering clear of all unnecessary skirmishes. The policy pays off. As others succumb to the conditions or mechanical failures, the Benetton B193B maintains its steady course and crosses the line in fifth place, albeit two laps down on the consummate winner, Senna.

Riccardo says: 'I'm sure the car could have raced faster, but mine was a tactical choice and fifth place means two points. That is not bad for the team. There are two ways to race in conditions like these – to attack or to defend and stay on the track. My results in South Africa and Brazil have not been brilliant. Under no circumstances could I have tolerated another negative result. I personally decided to run a safe race, relying on other drivers' errors rather than racing on the limit. In these conditions you can be happy just to cross the finishing line. It was terrible out there.'

The crew are weary and bedraggled. It has been an extraordinary afternoon. No one can recall a race with so many pit stops. The prospect of a hot bath and a hot meal sustains everyone through a working day such as this, and the Benetton boys still have work to do, clearing the garage and loading everything into the truck. It has not been an outstanding weekend for the team and no one is pretending otherwise. But the new baby should be stronger for the next race, and it is always the next race that matters.

■　■　■

Donington officials say they estimate the race day crowd at 50,000, which raises a few eyebrows. What everyone can understand is that Tom Wheatcroft has lost a lot of money on the venture. Usually reliable sources indicate he is down about £1 million on the £3.9 million outlay. Tom, though, retains the jovial countenance of a Dickensian benefactor. And he's even asking for more.

'It was worth every penny,' he says. 'Everything went against us. I never dreamt we'd have a wet practice day and race day. But if you look on the black side you'd never do anything. The drivers have voted it a success and we've had no red flags. I didn't want to say anything to FISA or FOCA about another race until I knew everything was all right at this one. Now I know it is I shall go to them and tell them we want more. I've turned everything in my life into a profit-making exercise, and I would this. I'm positive we can do a better job than Silverstone.'

It has, without doubt, been a memorable spectacle and Donington has perhaps won over a few new friends. There seems to be a growing consensus of opinion that the circuit deserves another shot. Certainly Benetton can sympathise with that 'it has to be better next time' feeling.

CHAPTER 6

PASTA AND POLITICS

The landscape is grey, desolate and inhumanly cold. It must be another Silverstone test. Riccardo Patrese and Michael Schumacher have barely had a chance to dry out after Donington, but they and the new car are back at work. Allan McNish joins them. Williams and McLaren are among the other teams here. There can be no let-up. Riccardo runs on the Tuesday until his engine capitulates. Michael is on duty Wednesday and Thursday, learning more about the B193B and bringing down his lap time to 1 minute 21.29 seconds. He is second fastest, behind Williams' Damon Hill, who clocks 1 minute 20.26 seconds.

Still there is more testing to be done before the San Marino Grand Prix, at Imola, on 25 April. The crew have two days at Pembrey, a track in South Wales, and squeeze in another stint at Silverstone, on Sunday morning, to run three cars which are to be transported down to Italy for the race.

All are anxious to take on board traction control, but despite the intensive testing they do not get the go-ahead. Frustrating though it is for Schumacher, he has to accept the decision that it is not yet ready for racing.

■　■　■

Breakfast up... Diana and Stuart Spires (bearded) feed the troops

Warm sunshine greets Formula One personnel to the Autodromo Enzo e Dino Ferrari, and there is a feeling that the season proper has arrived. We are into the European routine, at an established circuit, an outstanding circuit for that matter. This event is a convenient excuse for a second Grand Prix in Italy, though there is little early evidence of the famed passion for the sport here. Ferrari's demise – they face the prospect of a record 38th consecutive race without a win this weekend, on this, of all tracks – and a shortage of consumer cash are seriously affecting business. Some traditions endure, though, and pasta and politics are to be the order of this meeting, which is to prove dramatic even by Italian standards.

The ambience and colour of the paddock scene would lure the casual visitor into believing this is an idyllic village existence. Like all small communities, however, it is a breeding ground for petty jealousies and feuds and here, with stakes so high, the in-fighting can be savage. Benetton find themselves embroiled in a problem they did not anticipate, caused by confusion over the tyres they are allowed to use in qualifying. Schumacher is third fastest, behind the Williams pair, at the end of Friday's official practice session, and along with Patrese, who is seventh, he heads for a drivers v press charity football match content with his day's work.

Michael says: 'The team have made a very good effort today. We made some positive improvements during both sessions.' Riccardo senses an opportunity lost, saying: 'I was pleased with the car on my first run, but unfortunately there was some problem over which tyres we could use for the second set. By the time it was sorted out, the session was over.'

Schumacher returns from his football team's victory to be told he has more than just a problem over which tyres can be used. He is disqualified from the session. The Scrutineer's report states: 'During the first qualifying session the driver of car No. 5 used two sets of tyres which were of the same type as the evaluation tyres used by the same driver in the free practice this morning. This contravenes Article 103/C of the 1993 Formula One Sporting Regulations.'

The Stewards subsequently declare: 'Following Report No. 3 of the Scrutineers it was found the driver Schumacher infringed art. 103/C. After a regular inquiry and after hearing the Team Manager, the Stewards decided to cancel all the official times of the first practice session of driver Schumacher.'

Benetton are baffled and continue to plead that, as they read the regulations, they are not in the wrong. Ross Brawn explains that Michael felt the car was better on the B compound, a harder compound than the C, and that they were entitled to their preference. Comments from Goodyear lend support to Benetton's case. Flavio Briatore, Brawn and Gordon Message pursue a policy of quiet diplomacy.

Saturday morning, and the Stewards issue another statement. It reads: 'After having received new facts, hearing Mr Mehl, Competition Director of Goodyear, the Stewards carried out a supplementary inquiry of evidence and decided as follows – 1, From this moment onwards, the "E" marked evaluation tyres can no longer be used. 2, Therefore any driver can use a maximum of seven tyre sets (plus rain tyres without limit). 3, The exclusion of car No. 5 from the results of the timed practice of 23-04-93 is cancelled.'

Schumacher, reinstated, says: 'I am happy to see FISA are big enough to admit a mistake, and to change their minds and put it right. I hope it shows the way for the future.'

■　■　■

Tom Walkinshaw, meanwhile, has been leading the political battle on another front, and this is a complication that was envisaged. It is an increasingly vehement lobby from Ayrton Senna and his managing director at McLaren, Ron Dennis, for engine parity. Benetton are prepared to share the latest Ford Series V11 engines, which are theirs by contractual right, with McLaren providing they add their weight and expertise to a development programme through to the end of 1994. Most observers take the view that it is a totally reasonable proposition.

Schumacher gets the low-down from Ross Brawn (top) and Frank Dernie

The word around the paddock is that McLaren have two of the engines here, ready for use, but talks appear to have hit a snag. Senna, who has flown overnight from Brazil and arrives only five minutes before the start of practice on Friday morning believing the pressure tactics have worked, later accuses Benetton of moving the goalposts.

That is not quite Benetton's version of the situation and Walkinshaw, less than impressed with Senna's claim, calmly reveals behind-the-scenes events. He says: 'We were asked in October by Ford if we would consider their allowing Cosworth to supply McLaren with customer engines. Terms and conditions were worked out, we were happy, Ford were happy, and we signed. Presumably McLaren were happy because they signed a contract with Cosworth. It meant they would not have engine parity at all with Benetton for '93 and '94.

Above: Hot-shot... Schumacher's sights on another goal

Right: A bicycle made for two... Susi and Riccardo Patrese

'We had no pressure whatsoever from Ford Motor Company to amend that. They've made it quite clear that their contract with us is binding, and they are happy with that. If we wished to sit down with Ron Dennis and negotiate something, and it was to our advantage, they would have no objection. But at no time was there any pressure on us to do so.

'I met with Ron several weeks ago to go through the whole thing and I made my position clear to him. If he was prepared to sign up for 1994 and we jointly came up with a package whereby we could develop our '94 engine to a higher level of performance than it might overwise be, then I was prepared to sit down and renegotiate the terms and conditions of our supply agreement. He wasn't prepared then to commit himself through to '94.

'I foresaw exactly what has happened with Senna. I told Ford I expected it to happen at Donington Park. I was one race out, but it's happened. So I said, right,

we've got to try to resolve this one way or another, for one last time. We sat down on Friday morning, and I was prepared to negotiate on that basis. We met again in the afternoon, and I arranged for Ford and Cosworth to be available for a meeting on Friday night. I said I was prepared to sign if he was prepared to sign.

'Although he said in the morning he was prepared to do it, he now felt he was prepared to do it only if he had a get-out clause. He said he was happy to make the commitment, he was going to give me his word. I said, I don't know you well enough. I want it in writing. He said that if he put it in writing he wanted to be able to get out of it if he changed his

Top table talk... Niki Lauda, Consultant to Ferrari, Bernie Ecclestone, Formula One's impresario, and Flavio Briatore

mind. I said, what have you got in mind? He said he'd like to have a buy-out clause, a million dollars, to the end of the year. He said he was not going to just throw away a million dollars. I said, the trouble is, the development budget we're talking about is several million pounds. A million dollars is puny in relation to what we're putting in. The position was that if he wasn't prepared to do that there was no point in changing anything.

'As the meeting had been arranged with Ford and Cosworth senior management, I went back and saw them on Friday night to review it. Ron's plane was going to go back anyway to collect fuel and bits and pieces they needed to make up for the accidents they'd had and he said I could go in that. There was no point in two planes going back.

'So I went back in his plane and explained to Ford and Cosworth that we were back exactly where we were. I said, there it is, my position now is quite clear. I've tried everything. We'll respect the contract, Ford will do the same. McLaren will get the air valve engines in July, with the proviso that Ford and Cosworth supply us with the engine with the new cylinder heads.

'I can't see a deal being revived now. We can't re-run this soap opera at every race meeting. That's why I wanted this one effort. It was best for all sides to resolve it or agree not to resolve it right here and now. I said I would be happy whatever the outcome. The outcome was that McLaren would not sign up for '94, so we are abiding strictly by the contract we have.'

Walkinshaw, 45, has a reputation for strong leadership. Some find his very presence intimidating. He is built like the proverbial out-house and has a no-nonsense approach to racing and his many other business interests under the Tom Walkinshaw Racing banner. One of his former drivers in sportscars, Derek Warwick – not exactly a shrinking violet – named Walkinshaw as one of only two people who scared him. Warwick recalls an incident during his days with Jaguar (whose cars

Benetton's boys have all the angles covered

were run by TWR) when Tom turned up unexpectedly. He opened the motorhome door to see Warwick and the other drivers lounging about, feet up, their spent cups and cans scattered around the usually pristine retreat. Tom surveyed the scene, stony faced, and informed them he would be back. The instant the door closed Warwick and his colleagues, all experienced, internationally renowned racing drivers, jumped like scolded schoolboys and had the place back in order for the boss's return. (Incidentally, the other man who had that sort of effect on Warwick was another stickler for discipline and neatness, Bernie Ecclestone, President of FOCA and Vice-President of FISA.)

Tom, once a highly combative saloon car driver, revived the Jaguar racing tradition, taking them to the Sportscar World Championship and Le Mans success. Formula One inevitably beckoned, and he joined Camel Benetton Ford in 1991.

He says: 'I think anybody who manages a lot of companies has his own style, his own way of going about it. TWR consists of about 30 companies. You have to have your own systems that work for you and I have ones that work for me, and I have a lot of good lieutenants and managers who run the various companies and divisions for me.

'You have to be hard, uncompromising, but honest with yourself and acknowledge your strengths and your weaknesses. I have always tried to do that in my life. That's what I demand of my staff, as well. I'll sit down with them, try and identify the programme we want to follow, the pitfalls and our resolutions to them, and then I'll back them to the hilt until we deliver what we've decided we want to achieve. Obviously, if some people don't deliver what was asked of them or what they were committed to do, then you have to take the appropriate action.

'I've always been in businesses where you're driving things hard to deliver results in the time scale we've been given, whether it's engineering programmes, race programmes or whatever. So you have to be hard, you have to keep people's noses to the grindstone. But you get rewarded appropriately. We are in a high-risk, high-reward business. We have a salary structure which is considerably more than it would be for a like job outside the motor racing industry. It means people have to work long hours, work hard, and that's what they know they're signing up to.

'I don't see that it makes any difference whether you're a mechanic or a driver in that. You're a part of a team, whether it's a commercial team or a sporting team, and you've got to drive it through. Sometimes you have to drive people along by the scruff of the neck, so I suppose that's how you end up with a reputation that you are always hard. But I think I'm fair with people. I don't drive anybody harder than I drive myself, and I wouldn't ask anybody to do anything I wasn't prepared to do myself.

'I enjoyed driving, but I never did reflect that much after I had won something. I was more interested in the next one than sitting back basking in the glory of the achievement I had just accomplished. Delivering a result in touring cars is no more difficult or easy than here. It's just that it's different. You're taking on major motor manufacturers who are throwing all their resources at you, and you're starting with a compromise vehicle, something

Flavio Briatore and a welcome guest, Alessandro Nannini

that was designed for a totally different purpose, and having to turn it into a racing car, which is not easy. So each has its own, unique problem. The level of competition in Formula One is incredibly high, but again you probably have only three or four top teams and that's not really any different from any sport.

'I drove single seaters early in my career, but sponsorship in the early Seventies was impossible to obtain, and I was fortunate that Ford Motor Company wanted me to drive touring cars, and then BMW and others. I was being paid handsomely for doing that and I was good at doing that, so I made a career of that, and I have no regrets that I did.

'There is always the next programme, the next project. I'm involved in lots of interesting things, in racing and on the road. I enjoy taking on something new and doing it well. It doesn't matter if it's small or big. I get a buzz out of taking on something which is usually particularly difficult and delivering it within the parameters set out for it, whether budgetary or performance.

'The target here at Benetton is to do the best we can this year and try to finish in the first two in the Championship. We got off to an unfortunate start, what with races in the wet and a couple of slip-ups. We have a very technical car that was a bit late, but I think things will settle down in a couple of races and then it will be a good hard slog between us and McLaren throughout the year.

'We've got an engine that is probably worth about eight horsepower more than theirs, maximum ten, and they've got an engine that's got more torque than ours, so on some circuits their engine will probably be more suited than ours, on others ours will be better than theirs, performance-wise. That will be very interesting and I hope that the competition between the pair of us moves us closer to the Renault Williams.

'Our objective has got to be to beat Williams. I think we can only beat them this year, as has already been demonstrated, by putting pressure on them, by being close enough to force them into errors. Last year they were so far in front they could cruise through and do whatever they wanted to. They could always recover from it. This year it's a lot closer and they have to deliver a perfect race for themselves. If not, then we are close enough to get in front of them. I think that's the way it will be for the remainder of the year.'

■ ■ ■

The Camel Benetton Ford motorhome is a hive of activity all weekend. This is, after all, a team with Italian roots so interest is particularly intense. Flavio Briatore is a constant target for the media. He fields a stream of questions with patience and good humour. This may be the country where they change governments as regularly as Grand Prix drivers change tyres, but it isn't all about politics. The comings, goings and gossip are those of any village life – guests turn up for lunch, old friends pop in for a chat.

There is an especially warm welcome from the team and motorhome hosts Stuart and Diana Spires for Alessandro Nannini. The Italian's promising career as a Benetton driver was cruelly halted by a helicopter accident in 1990. His severed right arm was saved by hours of surgery and he has since returned to racing in touring cars. Here, he is working for Italian television. On screen and off, it's the same wide smile, the same charming manner they fondly remember at Benetton. He has a hug from Di. 'It's lovely to see him,' she says. 'He was always one of our favourites, one of the special ones.'

The Spires have been part of the Formula One cast since 1978, feeding, watering and counselling drivers and mechanics alike. They are Mum and Dad to their Benetton family, and to those who have, over the years, left the flock. A cuppa and a chat with Stuart and Di is a break to be recommended.

Di: 'I think we've become Mum and Dad of the team because we've been around so long. Most of the drivers who have worked with us here or at other teams call us Mum and Dad. Riccardo started calling us Mum and Dad the minute he arrived here. We are nearly a generation older than some of the new blokes around here these days, and some of the other motorhome people, who come round for a bit of help.

'If there is rivalry on the track there's none between the motorhomers. We are

The drama of the pit stop

all friends. You have to be. If you didn't help each other out you'd be in big trouble. Stuart is regarded as the sort of Dad of all the motorhome men. He helps with the parking in the paddock and they tend to come to him about the electrics and that sort of thing. It's grown from being a small job to a full-blown business for everybody. We started with Surtees, then Tyrrell, and came to Toleman when they were in Formula Two. We had two years at Lotus and came back here when they were bought by Mr Benetton.'

Stuart: 'We have two buses, this Benetton one and the Ford one. This is a full-time professional deal. We race, we test, we race, we test and we test all winter. Our home is in Alcester, near Stratford-upon-Avon, but last year we had, I think, 297 days away. We have a place in France and have spent one night there since Christmas. I can't see us doing another five years of this. In the old days it was definitely a sport and more enjoyable. Now there is so much more pressure on you all the time.

'The punters watching on TV think it all happens on the Sunday, but we usually arrive the previous Monday night and leave the following Monday. Tuesday is spent parking, titivating the inside, setting up the canopy, tables and chairs and plants. Wednesday is invariably a shopping day and the trucks arrive so we have the truckies to look after from that moment onwards. Thursday is the final titivation, so to speak, and the team usually arrive just after lunch-time so they want sandwiches already made up for them.

'The team alone here is something in the region of 50, what with mechanics, engineers and management. They have a full English breakfast, at lunch-time sandwiches, which are more time-consuming to prepare than cooking for them. They have their evening meals here on Friday and Saturday. The number of guests varies from place to place. There are some countries you'd think people wouldn't want to go to. Hungary is one of the busiest places for us, which I've always found quite amazing.'

Di: 'Over the years you get to know what you can buy from the local shops and once we've found out where things are, Stuart tends to do the shopping while I pre-plan a menu. It's nice to serve as much local food as we can and here in Italy most people like to have pasta. We've got four or five vegetarians in the team so we have to cater for them. Luckily, they all like pasta and salads, and they do eat cheese and eggs. They'll have vegetable lasagne, cheesy potatoes, that sort of thing, and lots of vegetables.

'Michael is guided by a dietician. He has muesli, vitamins, soya meat and vegetables, that sort of thing. Riccardo likes his Frosties and marmalade for breakfast, and pasta and bananas for lunch. Nelson Piquet used to have pasta and bananas as well, except that Nelson sliced the bananas on top of his pasta. Ayrton Senna had what we called the "Senna Sandwich" for breakfast when he was with us at Lotus. On a French stick he had ham, cheese and strawberry jam.

'Sandro took a liking to English breakfasts when he cut down on the espressos and stopped smoking. He used to have at least 12 espressos a day and was told that wasn't good for him. He would have a full breakfast, including what he called "special toast", which was fried bread. He had no idea what that was. But he'd ask for his breakfast at any time of the day, usually for lunch. When he was in hospital, after his accident, he said he couldn't wait to get back for his special toast, and the first meal he had was an English breakfast.

'I think you have to try to mother people in this job, and not only the drivers. It's the team, as well. I think it's because you're not a mechanic and not management, you're sort of always there and they tend to talk to you a lot. We get quite close to some of the drivers and they tend to come and sit on the kitchen stairs and have a chat, away from the management and the engineers, just for a bit of light relief.

'Nelson Piquet and Sandro Nannini, particularly, used to do that. Some you get more used to and closer to than others. Sandro, as I've said, was one and so was Nelson. Before Nelson came here to Benetton we'd heard he had a reputation for being a bit difficult and very outspoken, but our friends at Williams said you don't know him until you actually work with him. It's very true. He's just himself and one of the most amazing people, certainly among the drivers, that we've worked with. Sandro is so different and the two together were marvellous, such a good combination.

'We also got on very well with, and see socially, Thierry and Patricia Boutsen. We've known Nigel Mansell for over 20 years because he lived in the same area and we used to see Nigel and Rosanne socially as well. Even though he's gone to America we still communicate. I'd like to think we get on well with all the drivers. Some you get closer to, some are a bit withdrawn. They need to be with you a couple or three years but unfortunately they tend to move on. Gerhard Berger was very friendly but there was always that little bit of ... you were close but not that close. Ayrton Senna we go on quite well with.

'Riccardo has only just arrived but he's a perfect gentleman. He's very quiet, very nice, very polite. Michael's young and, yes, I would say he's far more relaxed than he was last year, far more chatty. He chats more with the boys. I think he had a lot of pressure on him last year but certainly I think this year he's more relaxed. When you've done a winter's testing with them, as we've just done, you get to know them a lot better because it is a lot more relaxed at testing.

Schumacher heads off Berger's Ferrari and the rest on his way to second place

'This year the engineers have a briefing room in their truck, so it gives the drivers a chance to relax more, which I do think they need, at least on race day, for an hour or so. Michael does like to relax quietly, not necessarily on his own but he prefers to be away from the engineers, just for that hour before the race, to play a bit of music and shut his mind off. He puts the headset on and lies down. He doesn't go to sleep but just relaxes, and it's good that they've got the space to do that. Martin Brundle, another driver we got on well with, used to lie down and go to sleep. Riccardo just seems quite relaxed anyway. I suppose it's because he's been around a long time and done so many races. He started around the time we did.'

Stuart: 'I have to say that recently we've had a few Italian test drivers and they are fantastic because they have not arrived yet, they are still trying to make it and they are not affected at all. Montermini, Zanardi, they are fantastic.'

Di: 'The younger ones are fresh and the pressure's not on them. They tend to be very friendly. Whether that wears off as they get further up the pecking order is another matter. Johnny Herbert is a near neighbour of ours and rings us up and we have dinner together. He and Zanardi make another good combination.

'One of the highlights for us was when Johnny had his first race for us, in Brazil in 1989. He'd had a really bad accident the previous summer and before the race we did a week's testing in Rio. He was told he would be allowed to race on condition that he completed a race distance in testing. He did that and came fourth in the race. It was quite emotional for everybody because we felt that we'd lived through all the pain that he'd had in his feet during the winter and during the test. It was one of those special occasions that always stay with you. And it's great, of course, when we win. We're part of the team and we feel we can share the win, as well.'

Stuart: 'I don't think we've had an occasion that's taken us to the brink. Well, we did have the occasion when we were the only motorhome at Ricard, in France. Elio de Angelis, whom we'd worked with at Lotus, was testing for Brabham. He and his girlfriend were sitting outside the motorhome, the sun was shining, it was a very pleasant day. His engineer came and told him his car was ready and off he went. His girlfriend stayed behind, having a soft drink. We all know what happened then. You can hear the cars, going round, then a bang, a pall of smoke, and then cars slowly drifting back. That was a horrendous occasion and it's strange how it affects you, you know.'

Elio de Angelis died the following day, 15 May 1986, from injuries sustained in the crash. He was 28.

Stuart: 'There was another occasion in our first year, when we were working for John Surtees. Ronnie Peterson was killed at Monza and one of the wheels came off his car and hit our driver, Vittorio Brambilla, on the head. It was touch and go whether he was going to be brain damaged. I have to say, though, that some thought he was brain damaged anyway! But Vittorio was one of the last characters of those days. To be honest, I think you come out of these experiences a little bit blasé. It says it on the ticket, doesn't it? Motor racing is dangerous. It's not nice when anything happens, but it's a job, isn't it? We all have to carry on.

'I don't think of anyone as a megastar. Motor racing is a great leveller of people. Whether you've got a million pounds or whether you've got nothing, if you haven't got a FOCA pass you are nobody. That's why I say, once you're in here it's a great leveller. We are all here for the sole purpose of racing and, hopefully, winning.'

Di: 'You do get people who don't really appreciate being here, people who don't realise how difficult it is to get them a pass. You see them sitting under the canopy all day, drinking, pass around their neck, and they've got no interest in what's going on. There are people out there who would give their life to come to a Grand Prix. I am actually a racing fan, otherwise I couldn't do this job. People ask why we do it and I suppose catering comes last. If you wanted to do catering you'd buy a restaurant, you wouldn't spend the amount of time away from home working the hours we do. You do 18 hours minimum a day, for five days solid, and you probably do a year's work in just over a third of a year.

'You couldn't do it if you didn't enjoy it. We had to choose the job or family and, luckily, we agreed on this. We haven't regretted it one little bit. We've seen the world, as much as you *can* see from a race track, and if it all stopped tomorrow, which can happen in motor racing, we'll have had a long and enjoyable run. Unfortunately, doing this job, I don't know what you can progress to. There's no tree to climb. You could come in in a managerial capacity with a couple of people working for you, but then I think you tend to lose a bit of contact. We've actually got three people working with us because Stuart's quite involved looking after the two buses – if the electrics go or the batteries are flat or something else goes wrong.

'I think when you don't enjoy it, it's time to stop. When you don't want to go to the first race and you know that you've got another 15, you've got to stop then. Hopefully, some time we'll strike the happy medium and live a bit in England, live a bit in France and perhaps go to a few races.

'It would be nice if, before we finish, we could win the World Championship. We've been very much a part of the team and Benetton has always been a team that make you feel part of it. We're like a big family because we spend so much time together. To win the Championship would be the ultimate, really. Then, I don't know. Retire, I suppose. We've been married 25 years, come some time between Japan and Australia.'

(Di is 45, Stuart 47.)

Stuart: 'A footnote – all I really want to do is sit on my little terrace in the sun, in the South of France, looking down the valley. How very pleasant.'

■　■　■

The sun continues to shine through Saturday but not, apparently, on Riccardo Patrese. He spins and slams into the wall at Piratella during the morning. The action is held up while the car and debris are cleared. Riccardo can manage only

Patrese monitors the progress of his rivals

11th fastest time in what is, for him, a truncated qualifying session. He says: 'The accident meant a lot of work for the mechanics and they got the work done about 20 minutes after final qualifying had started. Each time I tried to find a clear lap there was traffic or yellow flags or some other problem. Basically, a very frustrating day.'

Michael Schumacher is involved in another enthralling head-to-head with Senna, and again comes out on top. He will be third on the grid, behind the Williams Renaults of Prost and Hill. Michael says: 'I showed that we are capable of out-qualifying the McLarens. Ayrton and I had a good competition, and that is what the spectators want to see. Maybe I could have found another couple of tenths on my second set but I locked up my front brakes a couple of times and flat-spotted the tyres, so that spoiled my chances.'

Benetton are more than satisfied. Flavio Briatore says: 'I'm very pleased with Michael's grid position. He has had a lot of pressure one way or another all weekend and it's good to see him on the second row.'

Sunday morning is overcast and fresh. We have been told all weekend to expect rain and now we do. The weather is further dampening local enthusiasm for this event. The great hill which overlooks the bottom chicane is reasonably well populated, but in general the crowd is thin and cannot generate the vibrancy we associate with Imola. There is no sign of the scaffolding which is usually erected to provide makeshift stands for fans outside the circuit, or the foot clamps on perimeter walls. The 'tifosi' are at their lowest ebb.

The rain holds off for warm-up (Schumacher fourth, Patrese seventh) but arrives at 11.50. A 'wet warm-up' is called for, from 12.45 to 1.00 (Schumacher sixth, Patrese 12th). As race time, 2.00, approaches, the rain has all but ceased and that encourages the team. They are banking on a drying track and accordingly go with dry settings.

They start on wet tyres but expect an early change to slicks. For Riccardo it all becomes academic. He spins out at Tosa, the tight left-hander, on the first lap and cannot recover. 'I got a bump from behind,' he says. 'I tried to re-start but my engine stalled and that was it.'

Michael avoids trouble and has to bide his time, knowing that if the track does dry he will be in a position to step up the pace as the race progresses. He runs fourth and maintains his position through the flurry of pit stops for slicks. Hill's exit promotes him to third and he begins to chip at Senna's advantage. Then the Brazilian goes and he is up to second. Prost is well clear at the front and Michael is under no threat from Brundle's Ligier, so he settles for a solid second, the only driver to finish on the same lap as the Williams man.

Schumacher's exuberance on the podium reflects relief as much as pleasure. It has been that sort of weekend. 'Second place is good for me and the team,' he says. 'We have had quite a lot of pressure, so this should take away some of that pressure.

'During the first part of the race there was always a battle with someone either in front or behind me. I knew I would have to wait a while before the car would be really competitive. The wing settings we chose meant I was able to pull away on the straight, but the corners were a bit of a struggle. In the second half of the race the car was working perfectly. I was not pushing 100 per cent because I knew I already had a place on the podium. I was just taking care to finish. With the improvements we are making, more software and, of course, traction control, I think we can look forward to the next races.'

Schumacher celebrates with race-winner Prost

■　■　■

The rain may have relented for the drivers, but it has no sympathy for the mechanics. It is pouring down as they pack the cars and equipment into the trucks, which will be heading north, up the autostrada, in the morning. Another Camel Benetton Ford truck is parked just inside the circuit. It is the test truck, waiting to be moved into position for tomorrow. Yes, another test.

CHAPTER 7

FIGHTING FOR
THE CAUSE

Riccardo Patrese finds improvements at the Imola test and the search goes on at Silverstone. Still, though, the much-vaunted traction control is put on hold. It will not be used by Camel Benetton Ford for the Spanish Grand Prix, at Barcelona, on 9 May. Gordon Message says: 'It's working pretty well now but it's not quite... aggressive enough. Hopefully, Monaco.'

Michael Schumacher makes no attempt to hide his disappointment and hopes that rain – again threatened for race weekend – gives them a miss this time. Michael had a magnificent Grand Prix here last year, defying a downpour to make Nigel Mansell toil for his win in the unbeaten Williams. This year he would have to compensate for a further disadvantage.

■ ■ ■

Thursday 6 May, Circuit de Catalunya, and the rain arrives right on cue, greeting the teams as they saunter into the paddock, bags on shoulders, for the start of

The trials of the job...

another race weekend. If Michael is disappointed, Riccardo is positively agitated. The source of his displeasure is the speculation in the media about his future. Benetton are the latest team said to be interested in Mansell, his former team-mate now exiled in America. Riccardo says: 'I cannot understand why the press do not show me more respect. No, I have not so far driven as well for Benetton as I did at Williams, but I showed there what I can do and I shall do so here.'

Come Friday – a bright, sunny Friday – Patrese starts to make his point. He is running, it seems, more consistently, more confidently. Perhaps he is fired up. Certainly there is a sense of purpose and conviction about his driving today. He is fifth fastest in the free practice session and fifth again in qualifying. He says: 'I am quite happy with the car, although I think I need more grip out of the slow-speed corners. We will put that right tomorrow. Overall, there should be an improvement because I ran into problems with traffic on my last set this afternoon.'

Schumacher has a less comfortable passage through the day. He is troubled by some foreign body in his eye and takes a bumpy ride across a gravel trap during the morning session. He manages only 11 of the 23 laps he is entitled to, his best lap leaving him down in seventh place. He wastes no time getting to grips with the job in the afternoon. He takes fourth place on the provisional grid, behind Prost, Senna and Hill.

While Riccardo is on duty promoting the sponsorship involvement of Prince, the tennis equipment firm, Michael visits an eye specialist at a clinic in Barcelona. 'I got a tiny piece of carbon fibre or metal in the eye in the garage,' he explains. 'It was not the gravel. It was before then. It did not hurt but it was a little uncomfortable. Anyway, it had already gone when I went to the clinic. I have been given some drops and now I'm okay.'

His game of tennis that evening makes you wonder. He is given a 6-0, 6-0 thrashing by Flavio Briatore. 'I'm afraid I still have a lot to learn about playing tennis,' he concedes.

Schumacher and Patrese retain fourth and fifth places respectively on the second day, although the Italian is the more content of the Benetton drivers. He is less than a tenth of a second behind his partner. Patrese senses he has reached something of a landmark.

He says: 'This is the first time there has been no need for me to worry about staying on the road and not going off. I can feel the car – and it is good. For once I was able to think about being in front of Michael, even in front of Senna. After the first run this afternoon, the car felt good. So, for the first time this year, I went out on the second set and had confidence in the car. Until now, I have not been able to drive the car in the way that I know I can drive. This afternoon, I was able to attack.'

Schumacher does not have the same feeling. 'This morning,' he says, 'the car was nearly perfect, but for some reason it was quite different this afternoon. Something changed; I don't know what. There was a lack of grip in both the slow- and high-speed corners. For instance, the third corner I could take flat in the morning but it was impossible in qualifying. I should have gone a lot quicker. We will have to analyse what went wrong. Even so, fourth on the grid is a good place to start the race.'

An early start for the boys

■ ■ ■

Again this weekend, it seems much of the drama in Formula One has shifted backstage and, again also, Camel Benetton Ford are principal players and the focus of paddock attention. Apart from fielding questions about the connection with Mansell, Flavio Briatore is continuing to take a leading role in the campaign for cost-cutting measures which, he maintains, are essential to preserve the future of Formula One. There are meetings, and meetings about meetings. Even Luciano Benetton interrupts his tour of stores to drop in. He explains that Benetton have a 'responsible commitment' to Formula One, embracing a policy of reducing expenditure.

Luciano Benetton is a man constantly on the move. Often on foot. Rather than take a taxi between shops, he will walk, observing people, digesting styles and trends. In a restaurant he will study every diner. If a certain cut of cloth or hair, or a certain colour or combination of colours is in vogue in a particular locality, you can be sure he will have noted it and will brief his designers accordingly. His per-

Alessandro and Luciano Benetton

ception of Formula One is of a world which must learn to cut its cloth according to its means and give the customers the product they want.

He joins the team in the pit lane for free practice, then has talks with Bernie Ecclestone. Before resuming his tour, he offers his thoughts on the team he took over and the sport in which it participates. 'First of all I should stress that I play only a small part in the team,' he says. 'Flavio and Tom run the team and we have good people working here. I don't come to the races or get involved too much because this is their work. I always keep in touch, though, through Flavio or Alessandro.

'We thought of Formula One as the ideal vehicle for our company and then had the chance of a bigger involvement. Our experience of Formula One was zero but the Toleman team provided the solution. We hope our interest in the sport will endure a long time.'

Image is of paramount concern to Benetton and a balanced management of resources in Formula One is, he points out, consistent with the philosophy of his company. 'We feel very strongly about this issue. Formula One needs to lower its costs.'

The spectacles and tousled hair are an image of Benetton plucked from the posters. It is the casual, confident look of the casual, confident man and woman. And yet he is surprisingly quiet, almost shy and pointedly modest. He does not, for instance, gloat about his team's superiority over the team next door, Ferrari. Far from it. 'Ferrari are very important for Formula One,' he says, solemnly. 'We all need a healthy Ferrari. But it is hard for them. Unlike the other teams, they build their engines as well as their cars, which makes their task far greater.

'It is nice when we are competitive. We now have a good team. It is stimulating and prestigious, and I am very proud of the way Benetton Formula has developed and progressed. We are always aiming to continue improving and trying to be the best. And yes, to be champions. That has to be the ultimate ambition.'

■   ■   ■

The constructors meet that afternoon and into the evening to thrash out a technical formula for 1994. Despite the endeavours of Briatore and others, and a warning from FISA that changes would be forced upon them, they fail to reach agreement.

Some want active suspension and semi-automatic transmission to be allowed, some only semi-automatic transmission, others no technological aids at all.

Briatore regards this as further evidence that Formula One cannot move forward as it should when a unanimous vote is required to implement change. This vexed issue was central to his much-publicised confrontation with Williams during the winter. Flavio's business background and his extrovert style have inevitably aroused suspicion in the rather incestuous and protective environ -ment of Formula One, but there are those who believe his open manner and unconventional approach are refreshing and long overdue.

Briatore, 42, says: 'I am quite tired of all these meetings. People talk about the Concorde Agreement and how we need a 100 per cent vote to have any change. That is the first thing that is wrong. Surely a majority vote, a large majority, is sufficient. We have another good example with the meeting here. Nothing is decided. I still don't understand why we don't have a democracy in this place. Everybody speaks about my demonstration with Frank Williams as blackmail. It was not. I know it does not make sense to try to stop Frank being in the World Championship. I was making a point.

'I believe I approach this situation as both a businessman and a racing man. I try to see not only what is happening at Benetton but the overall situation. I believe we need everybody together, everybody involved and interested in Formula One, to make our business grow. This is my fight. It is always that, and not a fight just to gain an advantage for Benetton. You need everybody to grow. I see too many people with too much emotion and not enough of an overview of our business.

'I am very upset, very sad, when somebody tells me his team does not have the money, or the team manager has to mortgage his house to pay the debts. I don't think we should allow this situation. That is why I believe we have to fight this together. We need to be more optimistic, more positive, and give Formula One better PR. You never hear a driver say how wonderful Formula One is. Everybody complains. These people don't understand how lucky they are. You are doing the job you like, you make a lot of money and you don't promote your company. You complain, you spread rumour and everybody is discouraged.

'This is where the attitude of the press is also very important. The press goes for the bad angle and never the good angle. But I do understand when the press say Formula One is not open enough. We have a meeting, the press is not informed, so then you have rumour and speculation. I agree with the press there and I try to be open. The media is our partner and if you don't inform your partner what is happening, what can you expect?

'The fight for us is not about stopping active suspension or any particular thing like that. Honestly, I don't care about that. We have active suspension. Our business is big business, part of the world economy. When you have some indication the economy is changing you need to change before the market forces you to change. I try to look ahead, not back to yesterday.

'If you think of the flexibility we could have in our Association, with 10 people, but we don't use it. Somebody will say, I don't like to do such a thing because this guy is cheating. Those times have finished. That was 20 years ago, when six or seven people were in a team, and they could perhaps get away with a bit of cheating in the race. You can't cheat now, with 200 employees and a £20 million budget. People have changed their mentality. It's a commercial event. The race is part of the commercial event. If it was only the race, rather than spend £20 million you should spend £400,000 on a GT car, go racing and have fun.

'This is a tough business but I still have fun, absolutely. It depends how you conduct your business. From the communications point of view, I don't believe anybody here has anything to teach Benetton and I see, little by little, signs of change. I have been pushing over costs for four years and now everybody is a little more sensible about costs. I still believe it is possible to put on the same show for less money.

'This attitude where you spend a lot of money to make the car go faster, then a lot of money to make the car go slower, is crazy. You never finish and everything goes in the rubbish bin. People need to face reality and get their feet on the ground. If not, people will say to the sponsors, here are 20 opportunities, better than Formula One, for you to put your money in. But I believe there is no other sport like this if we handle the communications and the future as we should.

'I think people are bored by the technical side. What does the race mean? It means a fight between people. Now it looks like an engineering championship, not a drivers' championship, and you lose the reality. I don't have people stopping me in the street saying "Tell me, Flavio, what is the difference between your active suspension and Williams'? How many screws do you have in your traction control?" Nobody's interested. Everybody asks, "What happened to Patrese, what happened with Schumacher, what happened to Prost?" Why spend so much more on a product when nobody notices the difference?'

Mansell, of course, might be good for the show and it is no secret Formula One would like him back. Getting him back, however, may not be so simple.

Flavio says: 'People do not understand. They believe getting a driver is like shopping. You choose what you want, you put it in your basket and you take it home. It is not as easy as that. Sure, Nigel Mansell is a wonderful driver. But from what I hear, he has a very strong contract in IndyCars. I have a very strong contract with Riccardo Patrese and Michael Schumacher.

'Riccardo has had a problem with our car, in the way it is set up, and the way of working here. After changing things a little for Barcelona he is coming back into good shape. We had basically the same problem last year with Martin Brundle.

Facing page: Patrese on course for fourth place

The first four races were not so wonderful for him, but after that Martin had a fantastic season. You need time when you change teams, with the people and with the car.

'I can now see Riccardo becoming much happier. You could see it in his driving today. I don't think a driver like Riccardo forgets how to drive or take risks. You have to consider the different attitudes and approaches, depending on the characteristics of the driver concerned. It is like in business: everybody has his own approach in business.'

So what is Briatore's ambition for Benetton and Formula One? He says: 'My ambition for Benetton is to win. I came into racing to win. The trouble is that only one team can win. You see in the brochures of all the teams, even the last team, that things will be good and how next year they hope to win the World Championship. Only one team can be champions, as in any other sport, but it is possible for everybody to survive, if it is handled in a different way.

Patrese poised for action

'Benetton is very young and it is possible for us to do better. A lot of people are doing worse. I'm quite happy with the situation here. The difficult part for us is to go on now, take the next step and win the World Championship. But with the enthusiasm we have and a little creativity, I believe it will be possible. I feel part of the Benetton family, so for me there could be other challenges in the group, but here is the challenge I want.

'The challenge I see in Formula One is to get the sport doing business in the right direction and make sure we have competition between drivers. I want people to be waiting for Sunday, to switch on their television knowing it's going to be a good show. This is what I want.'

■ ■ ■

This show confirms Briatore's anxieties. There is an eerily subdued atmosphere about the whole Grand Prix meeting. The two preceding races here provided splendid entertainment, in keeping with an excellent circuit. Many of the modern tracks have been specifically designed with safety and close racing in mind. Too often, however, close racing means processional racing because circuits are so tight and twisty that overtaking opportunities are limited if not virtually eliminated. Barcelona is a welcome exception to the recent rule. The imaginative layout, with a variety of corners and a long straight for the authentic tow-and-pass manoeuvre, sets the drivers a genuine and invigorating challenge. The pits, paddock, grandstand and media facilities are of an equally high standard.

All the more depressing then that this event seems to be generating about as much fervour and public interest as a test session. The stands have been sparsely populated throughout practice and qualifying. Even along the pit lane, everything is strangely low key. The lack of atmosphere is a part of it, but also, the limit of 23 laps permitted each driver during free practice has taken some of the sting out of the session. Teams and drivers are able to go about their work at a distinctly more leisurely pace. It resembles a scene down at the local garage. Qualifying is tangibly more earnest and the real urgency, with three cars back in the equation, returns at Sunday morning warm-up.

On the roads leading to the circuit on race day, there is little evidence of urgency. What traffic there is flows freely and is soon parked. Morning rain is utterly appropriate. It is not what the Camel Benetton Ford camp want and senior management figures, gathered for breakfast beneath the motorhome canopy, step outside to take a look. Scowls all round. Michael Schumacher dashes across to the garage, bowl of muesli in hand. 'Senna must have been on his prayer mat again,' suggests an engineer.

Rain does appear to be Senna's only hope of retaining his Championship lead. By the end of qualifying he was well down on the Williams pair, Prost and Hill, and if the sun comes out again the chances are it will be a contest solely for the places. Those potential spectators who have stayed at home are fully aware of that, too.

By warm-up the rain has relented and the damp track will quickly dry. The order is the same: Prost, Hill, Senna, Schumacher, Patrese. For Schumacher, the target has to be Senna.

■ ■ ■

As the drivers make for their midday retreat, engineers and mechanics prepare the cars for a dry race. Management activity is centred on more meetings. Now Flavio Briatore is having talks with Duncan Lee and Richard Grundy, of R.J. Reynolds/Camel. Sponsors have to be updated on political and commercial developments. No one has unlimited funds these days and the companies who fund Formula One require assurances that the business is cost effective.

Punters may be thin on the ground but 'celebs' are in evidence here this weekend. George Harrison, ex-Beatle and long-time motor racing fan, has made one of his occasional visits to a Grand Prix. Motor cycling has a far bigger following in Spain and some of its protagonists are here. Sightings so far include Kevin Schwantz, Kenny Roberts, Alex Criville and Sito Pons. Also on view – though here strictly for the Porsches – is Brigitte Nielsen. Always good for a few gags about active or passive suspension ....

The mood at Benetton appears cheerful, too. Michael has his sunshine, Riccardo has the signs that his form is returning, and Flavio has the chance to light up a cigarette.

■ ■ ■

At two o'clock the 25 qualifiers meander around the 2.95 Circuit de Catalunya on their parade lap. They crawl on to the grid, pulling out of single file to take their positions in the staggered formation. All are in place ... red light on ... a crescendo of engine noise ... and flashing amber! The two Williams and the McLaren of Senna – who swears he saw green – are instantly away but others, including Schumacher, hesitate. Instinct takes over and fortunately they get off safely.

Schumacher retains his fourth place, Patrese his fifth, and they settle down behind Hill, Prost and Senna. Hill gives way to Prost at the end of the straight, on the 11th of the 65 laps; otherwise the leading pack hold station into the second half of the race. At the end of lap 37, Michael heads for the pits, 'I began to get a vibration from the tyres. Then the gearbox seemed to develop a mind of its own. It went down to first and then into third when I was not expecting it. So I thought a change of tyres might cure the gearbox problems because it would get rid of the terrible vibration.'

He re-emerges still ahead of his team-mate and, equipped with fresh rubber, sets about bridging the gap to Senna. The incentive for the chasing pack is sharpened when Hill, after threatening to regain the lead from Prost, is forced to retire on the 41st lap with a blown Renault engine. Schumacher builds up his momentum, despite more problems. 'The gearbox worked all right for only about five laps after the pit stop. Every time I went to use second gear, the box went into first. So that meant I could only use third where I really needed second.'

The problem scarcely cramps his style. He records the fastest lap on the 48th and again on the 50th. Senna responds on lap 52 by diving into the pits for new tyres. His strategy almost backfires when mechanics struggle with the rear left and, to his undisguised frustration, he loses precious time. Schumacher, smelling a possible second place, launches a ferocious assault with a succession of fastest laps. At the end of the 53rd lap the McLaren and the Benetton are separated by eight seconds. At the end of the 54th it is seven seconds.

Senna, his tyres now warmed up, retaliates. He reduces the fastest lap time on the 56th. Schumacher counters: a new fastest lap time on the 57th, and on the 58th, and on the 61st. Now he has Senna firmly in his sights. The gap is down to 2.6 seconds. Five laps remain. Schumacher has breathed life into an ailing race.

As they approach the end of the 62nd lap, it appears he may get a helping hand from the traffic. Alessandro Zanardi's Lotus Ford is in Senna's path. The Brazilian gets round, leaving Schumacher to track the Italian through the final corner of the lap. Then Zanardi's engine blows, forcing Schumacher to run wide.

Michael finds himself on the grass and does extraordinarily well to wrestle the Benetton back on to the tarmac. He is still in the race but, sadly, out of the scrap for second place. He has to content himself with third.

He says: 'There was a stage when I thought I would not make it to the end, never mind finish third. I nearly lost it a couple of times and when Zanardi's engine blew up in front of me I could hardly see for all the smoke and oil. I knew he was still on the line so I pulled out wide to pass him, but when I turned the wheel the car went straight on. After that I was quite happy just to keep the car on the road and bring it home. I think I have been lucky in Spain. I have always finished in the points here and this is another good result for me and the team.'

So is the fourth delivered by Riccardo, who has also had to contend with a vibration. He says: 'The car was working very well but we had a vibration problem yesterday and again this morning during the warm-up. We didn't manage to cure it. My car was vibrating a lot at the end of the straight and I had a problem with my left front wheel. I had chosen not to push too hard at the beginning because I wanted to finish the race without changing my tyres. I am happy. It is a positive result.'

That is how Flavio sees it: 'A good result for the team and an exciting race for us as Michael chased Senna. It's good for Riccardo, too. We're very pleased for him.'

The result lifts Prost above Senna to the top of the World Championship and Schumacher above Hill to third place. Riccardo is joint seventh and Benetton are third in the constructors' standings.

Michael takes the opportunity to return to a subject close to his heart – traction control. He says: 'We have been asking for traction control since the end of last year, ever since we knew in which direction we were going with the car and the technology. I thought we would have had it for racing some time ago, but we are still being told to wait until the next race. This is very frustrating. One of the main reasons for this is that we have developed a specific type of traction control which does not work through the ignition or fuel systems but through the throttle. It is more complicated than earlier systems used in Formula One, but the team believes that it will save on engines. This is important to us as a team, and, of course, to Ford.

'The effect of not having traction control has been clear for everyone to see in the wet races this year and it is for that reason that I am pushing hard now. We have to push as hard as possible so that we will have it ready for Monte Carlo, where it will really matter in the race. The advantage of traction control varies from circuit to circuit. In Barcelona, in the dry, for example, I would say it is worth around three-tenths or four-tenths of a second a lap. At Imola it was worth about six-tenths in the dry and 1.5 seconds in the wet. It is the main area in which I feel we have been missing something to maintain our competitiveness in the last few races.

'Monte Carlo is a circuit where traction control will be vital. If we do not have it, we will not be totally competitive. I am talking about beating McLaren and that is a realistic target. When we have done that, then we can aim for new targets.'

CHAPTER 8

FACES OF A CLASSIC

There are, as we shall discover, many faces of Monaco. The face which greets the Formula One roadshow is wet and solemn. Every now and then the rain goes up a gear, sending team personnel scurrying for cover under awnings and makeshift shelters. Everything about this circuit is temporary. The barriers go up around the streets of the Principality just for this weekend and teams have to contend with the worst facilities on the tour. The cramped pits area cannot accommodate the now standard garage requirements, so the crews have to set up separate compounds down by the paddock, which is perched on the quayside several hundred yards away. Such a tight, twisting track and such spartan working conditions would not be tolerated anywhere else. The authorities argue that it is worth making an exception for the Monaco Grand Prix, and even the drivers agree. No other race has the same aura, the same prestige or the same capacity for generating money. Those qualities are permanent, as, it seems, is the event's place in the World Championship. So is the first day of practice here: Ascension Thursday. The Friday is consequently a rest day.

German heroes... footballer Thomas Doll meets Michael Schumacher

Wednesday's rain, and the forecast of more to come, fills the teams with trepidation. There is, though, some consolation for the Camel Benetton Ford drivers, Michael Schumacher and Riccardo Patrese. Their B193Bs are at last equipped with the throttle intervention traction control system and its benefits will be appreciated all the more if the track is wet. With top-end power not so significant on this circuit, Benetton have decided to use an earlier engine specification, which they believe will complete a more effective package here. Flavio Briatore, moving smartly out of the deluge to take sanctuary beneath the motorhome canopy, says: 'Now we have the same power as McLaren, so we shall see if there was such a big difference before. I tell you, it was next to nothing.'

Rain clouds are still clinging to the mountains surrounding Monte Carlo on Thursday morning. This is not the vision we see in our imagination, but it is the intimidating reality. There is a reprieve for the start of practice, yet still the track is damp.

Patrese, after an early run, returns to the pits to express his dissatisfaction with the road-holding of his car, and adjustments are made. His problems are insignificant compared with Ayrton Senna's, in the McLaren Ford. He loses control approaching the first corner, Ste Devote, smashing into the barrier on the left, bouncing across the road and hitting the one on the right. The impacts rip off the left side and nose of the car, leaving the Brazilian badly shaken and nursing an injured left hand. Schumacher takes a look down the escape road at Mirabeau and has a spin as the rain returns, finishing the session in tenth place. Patrese is fifth.

Schumacher goes straight on at Mirabeau again during qualifying, as this teasing circuit continues to play tricks with the drivers. It is drying, but only very slowly. Michael briefly moves up to second place and is third at the end, behind the Williams pair, Damon Hill and Alain Prost. Riccardo is sixth, immediately behind Senna.

'The traction control works fantastically well,' says Michael. 'We can be very happy with our achievements today. All credit must go to our engineers, considering it's the first time we have used it. It gives me great confidence and with this system there is a lot of potential for more development. I was lucky to finish the session because I had a bit of a problem with the throttle. On my first lap, the engine just stopped. I put my foot on the clutch and let it go down the hill to Mirabeau. When I tried again, I released the clutch and the engine started. There were a couple of moments when I touched the barrier. But it was a good performance today and even in the dry we should be able to retain a good position on Saturday.'

Riccardo says: 'We have a lot of new things on the car here and it takes time to find the best set-up. But already we know what to do if it is dry on Saturday. The important thing today was to set a reasonable time for the grid without having any problems. Of course, if final qualifying is dry then we have to do it all over again, so there was no point in taking a big risk today. As for the traction control, that helped a lot in these conditions and now we can really attack the opposition.'

■　■　■

Another face of Monaco appears on Thursday evening. It will be in evidence deep into the night, through Friday, and doubtless again on Saturday night and, for the really durable, yet again after Sunday's race. This is the face of the party-goer. The party-goer may be a parody of himself or herself these days, and tell you it's not what it used to be. Certainly the drivers are not so much in evidence in the bars and clubs as they used to be, but then all sports people are more serious and dedicated now. The younger revellers, however, still have fun, even at Monaco's outrageous prices. This is, after all, a special kind of bash and the punters come suitably prepared.

It is a time for dressing up and plain showing off; it is a time to have that occasional flutter at the Casino; it is a time to pull every trick in the book to get yourself an invitation on board one of the yachts ostentatiously moored within the arc of the circuit. This is the shop window, the opportunity to impress would-be sponsors or keep existing backers sweet. It is a time to meet old friends and make new ones. Monaco reunions are part of the ritual at this uniquely extravagant event.

For those energetic enough, there are sporting diversions on the Friday. The sun is up and so are some of the drivers to have an early round of golf. Schumacher and Patrese join the other Camel-sponsored drivers, Prost and Hill, at a press lunch before making their way to the Benetton/Prince tennis tournament at the Monte Carlo Country Club. Michael, as he has already explained, is still learning the game and goes out in the second round. Riccardo sets his sights rather higher but, to his undisguised dismay, loses his semi-final tie against Flavio. Alas for Flavio, he too meets his match in the final. He is done to a turn by the Ford motorhome chef, fellow Italian, Luigi Montanini.

The day is warm and here, at last, is the face of Monaco everyone recognises from their television screens. Bare-chested British and German fans sprawl in chairs at pavement cafés, downing lagers, reconstructing the grid for Saturday, plotting every move in the race. Others hover around the motorhomes, hoping for a glimpse of a driver, an autograph, even a picture and a chat with their favourites. There are always show-business folk and personalities from other sports around, too. It is a people-watchers' paradise.

■　■　■

Mechanics and engineers are also down by the waterfront on this sunlit Friday. More specifically, they are in their individual team compounds, working on the cars. The pace is comparatively leisurely, partly because there is no practice today so they have no need to rush, and partly, one suspects, because there may be one or two delicate heads this morning. The rest of their weekend here is more fraught, even by Formula One standards. Two of the Benetton mechanics, Kenny Handkammer and Andrew Alsworth, introduce us to yet another aspect of Monaco, their Monaco, the face washed of its glitz and glam.

Handkammer (the name, coincidentally, is German) works as No. 2 mechanic on Schumacher's car. 'I'm basically responsible for the back end – gearbox, rear suspension,' he says. 'I've been with Benetton four years. Before that I was with a Formula 3000 team. I've been a mechanic for the last seven or eight years. Before that I ran a company for my brother, in engineering manufacturing. I came into this because it was something I wanted to do. There was a position available in a racing car company; I applied and got the job. There used to be a frustrated racing driver in me, but not now. I think I'm too old. I'm 28.'

Alsworth, 32, is the team's spares man. He says: 'I've been here eight years. I was with British Leyland making prototype cars and then saw an ad in the paper for Toleman. I went to work in the composite department, which was new. Their chassis was made outside until then. I worked there for three years, then on assembly as a mechanic, and then the spares job came up. Basically, we take two sets of car spares for three cars. When the cars are travelling in the trucks, there's still a lot of stuff being produced in the factory which we have to take on the plane as hand baggage.'

Kenny: 'People back home seem to think we lead the life of Riley, with all the travelling and so on. From the outside it must look like that, but it's not really.'

Andrew: 'Yeah, you go down the pub and everyone says they saw it on the telly and what a good job we've got. But the hours we do...'

Kenny: 'I think we've done 100 to 120 hours a week in some cases, building the car up and testing. I've worked all night, something like a 48-hour shift for instance, several times. I'm not married and I'd say it's definitely not a job for a married man. There are a lot of married guys here and I don't know how they do it.'

Andrew: 'I'm not married and I'd agree with that.'

Kenny: 'This is the hardest race for us. The basic problem is that we haven't got a proper pit area to work from. As you can see, we have to work under the awning here, and then, early each morning, take everything up to where we run. It's not just the cars, it's everything else – tools, spare bodywork, the lot. So it means the truckies have a particularly hard job of it, getting all that stuff up there. You've got to look after it all while it's up there, then bring it all back down again after the session. By then there's hundreds of people around and it's chaos.'

Andrew: 'The pit lane is dangerous. If you are not aware of where you are and where the lines are, it's really dangerous. It's narrow, it's congested and it curves, so you can't always see cars coming in. Last year Mansell came in late for tyres and if anyone had stepped out he would have had them. Yesterday it rained – you've got oil etc., so it's even more uncomfortable and dangerous. There's also the security problem. Things get pinched. You have to say that it's not really fit for a Formula One race.'

Kenny: 'I think they could do a bit more to make it better. At least if you could have the cars up there all the time it would help. It doesn't have to be that big an area. It would be so much easier if you had the trucks down here and the rest of the stuff up there.'

Andrew: 'It's easier than it was four or five years ago because the team is a lot more aware of what they've got to take and are better organised. We have lists displayed on the van: take that, unload it, that comes back, etc. We're lucky we're down here. This is a big result for us. We used to be up on the top road there with the other smaller teams. Alcatraz, we call it. It's terrible.'

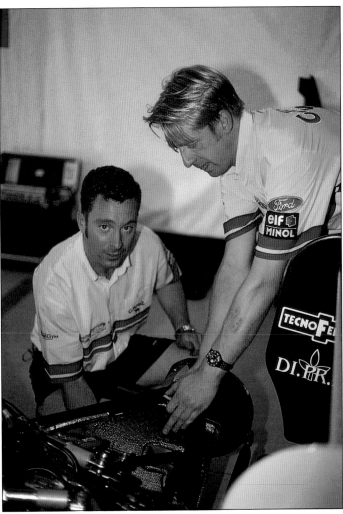

Kenny Handkammer (left) and Andrew Alsworth

Surely, though, it's not all hard labour? The lads must escape Alcatraz and all the other compounds on Thursday night, don't they?

Kenny: 'We stayed in the hotel to start with, then went down to a local bar for a few beers. It's a bit pricey here, though. Monaco just stinks of money, doesn't it? We are quite lucky because our hotel is half-board, so we get an evening meal. If you have to eat out every night it gets very expensive.'

Andrew: 'It's pretty good money we're on and we get £27 a day expenses for two days, then £10 a day for the next two days because we get fed by the motorhome personnel. We used to be on a bonus system and that's a bit of a sore point. Last year everyone at the factory got £35 a point. We got 91 points so we had a good Christmas.'

Kenny: 'As the cars were finishing in the points, we were counting the money up through the year. It's a big incentive, for sure. But, what with recession and everything, I suppose there's not as much money around. I'm still happy to stay in the job for a while. I enjoy it. Obviously the drivers are well paid because they take the risks, don't they? I think some of the big money, the 12 million dollars some get paid, is obviously ludicrous. You can argue until you're blue in the face about what a driver is worth, but 12 million dollars, I mean, that's half your budget gone on wages.'

Andrew: 'I think one of the good things here is that we all get on really well. I think we get on better than any other team of mechanics. We get on with other teams as well. There's friendly rivalry between us. I think we're all mates and we'll have a drink together.'

Kenny: 'You'll hear about some teams where guys working on a certain car are told not to go and speak to that guy on the other car. But we're okay all the time. There's no rivalry between the different sets of mechanics.'

Andrew: 'There's a good atmosphere between the drivers and mechanics here, as well. The drivers just seem to fit in. Michael's good and Riccardo is always around. Nelson and Sandro were very good, too. Michael came out with us to one of the islands off Australia for a holiday at the end of last season. We played tennis, went scuba diving, that sort of stuff. He's three hours down the gym every day. He's got a brilliant physique. He's taken fitness to a new dimension. Having said that, Riccardo went for a run the other day and I've never seen back muscles like he's got. It's handy, finishing the season in Australia. Usually we get to Bali or somewhere. Between Japan and Australia we went up to the Mirage at Port Douglas. Five days we had there. Six of us. Brilliant. No birds, of course... '

Kenny: 'The bash between Australia and Japan is the one everyone looks forward to because the company pays for it and we obviously have a good time. It's only four or five days but it's great. We take our actual holiday at the end of the year.'

Back to drivers. What type of driver do you prefer and who's the best around?

Kenny: 'The right type of driver is a difficult thing to gauge. You can have someone who's very young, hot-blooded, who's probably going to drive his boots off. But then you've got another guy who's not going to push until it's perfect, and that helps a team more because instead of driving round the problems, the problems get solved and that helps everybody. Michael's very quick, but he's 24, he's had only one season in Formula One and there's more to come from him. He knows that himself. At the moment he's doing a fantastic job.'

Andrew: 'There aren't that many good cars around so who knows what the other younger drivers could do, given the opportunity. Senna's still the best, though. I think most of the other guys will tell you that.'

Kenny: 'If anyone will throw in an unbelievably quick lap when he has to, right at the very end, it will be Senna. Some drivers you like, some you don't, just like

Facing page: A winding path to disappointment for Patrese

any other normal human beings, you know? I think they appreciate what we do and the effort we put in.'

Andrew: 'When Michael goes up on the rostrum he's the only driver who looks as if he's had a good day. Senna and the rest of them don't look as though they enjoy it the same. Even for a third place, it means a lot to him, and that makes us feel good. It's a team effort. There's not just one component that makes him successful – it's the whole team. Now I'd like to win a few more. We've got so much

The new Prince of Monaco?

new stuff on the car, which Williams have had a couple of years, and it's going to get better, I think, this season.'

Gordon Message can still relate to the life of a mechanic. You sense, observing him, talking to him, that he would prefer to be just one of the boys. At heart, he probably still is. He says: 'I feel guilty if I go home when the guys are working late at night or all night. I try to stay there. I generally do. Then, when we get back from the races, I've always got something to do. I enjoy sailing, but I don't get to do much of that. There's been a lot of hard work for all the team.

'I was always a racing fan. I wanted to drive, that's all I wanted to do. I did a bit of driving, but only karts, really. I've done some motocross, that sort of stuff. I started as a mechanic when I left school. My parents were quite keen that I did some sort of recognised apprenticeship. I wasn't interested in general engineering, it had to be some type of mechanical engineering. I did an apprenticeship at a Vauxhall dealership in Chislehurst. It was the beginning of 1977 I started this. I went from March to Toleman and I've been there ever since.

'I've gone through the various changes with the team and, to be quite honest, I preferred working for a smaller team. You're more involved in lots of things, you've got your finger on the pulse. It's much more difficult to do that now. There are so many people involved and responsibilities get split and fairly well defined. It's different, vastly different from my early days with Toleman, that's for sure.

Gordon Message

'I think I'm essentially the same bloke and maybe I shouldn't be. Maybe I should have changed. But I find that quite hard and I don't really want to change. I made a conscious effort not to become one of those people I didn't like when I was one of the boys, if you understand. I'm not so much one of the boys now but half and half. I'm right in the middle, whereas I should be completely separated, I suppose, to get any further. But I'm quite happy, really, where I am.

'It helps dealing with the boys and I don't have any problems with them. I know what they do is difficult because I've done it myself. I know how they feel sometimes and understand when they react accordingly. I don't think it's harder being a mechanic these days. As I've said, the team is much bigger and their responsibilities are more clearly defined. When I was a mechanic we had to build our own gearboxes, suspension components, everything. Against that, this active suspension and all the electronics and hydraulics that go with the car these days are much more complicated than anything I had to deal with, so it probably evens itself out.

'As team manager, I'm responsible for a lot of logistics, planning and arrangements for the race weekend. It doesn't really make any difference whether it's a European trip or long-haul. The only difference there is that the freight goes by plane to the long-distance races and by truck to the European ones.

'This year has been one of the hardest because we've had so much to do over the winter. We've been developing the automatic gearbox, active suspension, and various other projects. We've been doing a massive amount of testing, a lot of which can't be planned much in advance because we have to react to certain problems and developments. The guys understandably get a bit uptight because they don't know what they're doing. Some of the race team have to go testing, some of the test team have to go racing. For the married guys it can be particularly difficult.

'It's certainly less fun than it was, but then the whole thing is more serious than it was, say, 10 years ago. I remember our chief mechanic of a while ago having this thing about Superglue and the things we got up to with this Superglue you wouldn't believe. One incident which does stick in the mind (no pun intended, honestly) was when we managed to secure the then team manager out of his room in rather embarrassing circumstances.

'For the past couple of years I don't seem to have had any time for social functions that the drivers might have been at. That's a sign of the times, I suppose. The drivers are busier than they have ever been with sponsors' commitments etc., and that is very much a part of the business these days. On the driving side, they need the car in which to perform. The car is the concept of the technical director or chief designer and I think the balance in salaries between the drivers and technical staff is slightly wrong. We don't dispute the drivers are very good at what they do and that they are the ones taking the risks out on the circuit, but a lot of effort goes on behind the scenes from people who couldn't care less about the money. I agree with drivers' salaries being pegged a bit. They've been getting out of hand, for sure.

'I think people in the outside world would be surprised at the commitment from so many people within a team. I'm not saying there aren't people out there in normal jobs who don't give an awful lot of commitment; I know there are. But this is just so demanding for everybody involved, especially at specific periods. That's why I class this as an abnormal job. It takes a special animal to want to do it and stick at it. It's a love of what you are doing, it's a love of the sport because, at the end of the day, you wouldn't put up with all the aggravation for any other reason. It's the satisfaction of seeing what you've been doing over the last week or two actually working on a circuit the following weekend. The ultimate satisfaction of my life would be to see Benetton win the World Championship.'

■　■　■

Those who survive the ordeal by Tip Top, Rosie's and sundry establishments offering similar refreshments blink their eyes to a warm, sunny Saturday. Some may even recall that Formula One practice resumes this morning. Ah yes, that! Schumacher is certainly up for it, here at his adopted home. His exuberance, however, is shackled by a series of problems: an oil leak, gearbox and active suspension gremlins, and the odd spin. He finishes the unofficial session sixth. Patrese has a less complicated stint and completes the exercise fourth fastest.

By the afternoon Michael's mechanics and engineers have done their stuff and the No. 5 Camel Benetton Ford looks in menacing form. Prost, patently happier on the dry road, sets the target for the rest to aim at. Senna's first run takes him to second place. Hill, the provisional pole holder, registers third quickest time. Schumacher flexes his muscles to go fifth, then delivers a crunching blow to Senna. The German is second, the Brazilian third. Senna responds with inevitable aggression, only to lose the McLaren coming down the hill to the chicane and spin into the escape road. Schumacher confirms his front-row place by further improving his time. Qualifying is less productive for Patrese, who will line up sixth on the grid.

Riccardo makes no attempt to mask his disappointment. He says: 'I had too much traffic on my first set of tyres and that meant I had to do an extra lap, which I had hoped to save for my second set. When I went out on the last set, for some reason the tyres did not reach the ideal working temperature.'

Michael's mood is entirely different. He has had an excellent afternoon and feels his relentless nagging for traction control has been proved justified. 'This afternoon was an extremely smooth session for us,' he reports. 'We experienced no further gearbox or throttle problems. I have to thank the team because the effort put in since Barcelona has been outstanding. We also made considerable changes between the two sessions, which worked really well.

'The car has more mechanical grip with the active system and now the traction control. I had the pleasure of trying the traction control in the morning because we had to do something else, so I had to switch the traction control on and off. Just by doing this I got 1.2 seconds! It is a big difference. It gives you so much more confi-

dence that you drive completely differently. This is the main point and how you improve the time. Now,' he adds ruefully, 'I can imagine what would have happened if we had had it before...'

From the backward glance, Michael soon has his eyes on the road ahead again. 'I think to be on the first row has to be good,' he says. 'Now we have the package a lot better and I think there is still a lot to come. I am really looking forward to the race tomorrow. I shall be happy when the start is over and to run in second place for a while, leaving Alain to take the pressure!'

Schumacher is intoxicated by the Monaco Grand Prix. 'Driving here is something different from normal circuits, where you have more freedom and feel a lot safer,' he says. 'It is something completely different and I don't want to miss it. The atmosphere is fantastic, a real racing atmosphere, as it should be. The last race, in Spain, was like a test session compared with this. I want to see more circuits like this. They are more tricky and you can get more out of your car.'

Michael has become something of an ambassador for Monaco. Almost half the drivers have places here, though not all are as conspicuous residents as the younger Benetton driver. Riccardo, for instance, also has a home in the Principality but remains devoted to Padua. Michael has taken the decision to live here. He and his girlfriend, Corina, have an apartment in Fontvieille. 'We are opposite the supermarket, which is very convenient,' he says. 'I like the quiet area, which is why I live there. You cannot hear all the noise of the town of Monaco. In fact, all you can see is ships and water. It is nice, this weekend, to be able to go home at night to my own bed, and have my own bathroom and breakfast in the morning. I can escape.

'I moved here last year, but not, as everyone supposes, just to join up with the many drivers who live here. It was a logical decision for business reasons and it has worked out very well. In fact, I believe I now spend more time visiting my family and friends than I was ever able to do when I was still living at home in Kerpen. I had lost my normal lifestyle in Germany, anyway. When I was at home, I didn't feel I was at home at all. I had so much work to do and there were always interruptions and demands on me. Here, no one makes a fuss. I can live a normal life again. I am able to enjoy a good climate and lifestyle. I feel very settled, and so does Corina, despite the fact that we had our Mini stolen. That was a bit of a shock, but one we have got over.'

(It may also have spared him further sabotage at the grubby hands of his team. That old black Mini was a sitting duck for mechanics in a restless, mischievous mood at a test session at Paul Ricard. They dumped rotten fish in the boot. Michael also discovered his clothes wrapped around the Benetton antennae, on the pit wall. Michael, who is known to have an able accomplice in his physio, Harry Hawelka, retaliated with similar pranks, including the old slap-the-eggs-in-the-pockets routine. His victim was test driver Zanardi, an equally guilty party in all these shenanigans.)

'I bought a Ford Escort, which is ideal for Monte Carlo, where parking is always a problem, and now I have a 750cc motorbike, which I really like. Now, for the summer, we hope to spend time in a water-ski boat, but I shall not be doing the skiing. Corina will do that, while I shall be in the boat. It is the ruling for drivers: no karting, which is really my hobby, or skiing, except in the winter.

'In Monaco I am able to work much better on my conditioning than I would be able to in Germany, particularly through the winter. I am a regular at the Loews gymnasium and often work out with friends or other drivers, particularly Aguri Suzuki. Finding the right routine and fitness levels is very important for a driver today, given the amount of physical stress we have to undergo in a race and the high level of G-forces. It is good to have the company of another driver in training as we do similar work, although Aguri does a lot of running while I do a lot of bike work.

'Apparently there have been stories in the newspapers that I have big problems with my knee and that I am only just able to drive. It is true that I have had some trouble with the knee and it has been affecting me for some weeks. I am not sure exactly what it is but it is sometimes quite painful. I notice it most when I am running or playing football. I think it may be a slight cartilage or ligament problem. This is why I do cycling instead of jogging. It is not too serious but enough to worry me a little and I can feel it in bed when I am trying to sleep, too. I guess I will have to see a specialist at the end of the season. I think I may have strained my knees when I was younger, doing a lot of weight work and squat-lifts. Thankfully, it is not a problem for me in the car. I suppose it is just one of the problems of getting old!'

■　■　■

Sunday 23 May: race day. Still the sun is shining, although a few clouds are drawn to the mountains. 'It should stay dry, but you never can tell at Monaco,' says one old sage, peering from the Ford motorhome. A dinghy pulls up in front of the Benetton motorhome, next door. Flavio and Tom clamber out and onto the quayside. They seem cheerful enough, and so they should be. There is an air of expectancy in the camp.

All around Monte Carlo there is a buzz. Michael is right. This place is different. It may be illogical to run a Formula One race on streets of such configuration and dimensions, but look at the result. This is the blue riband event and nowhere do the spectators get closer to the action. Already they are filling the stands, clinging to vantage points at Tabac and Casino Square, and high up on the hillside overlooking the last corner. Every balcony with a glimpse of the circuit is occupied, even those up in the old part of town. The acolytes and sycophants preen themselves for this race as for no other, but they do not always come properly equipped. One VIP turns up without his pass and tells his sponsor: 'I didn't think I'd need it.' That pass is worth a small fortune.

Schumacher leads much of warm-up, but Prost again goes top. They finish as they finished the final qualifying session: Prost first, Schumacher second, Senna third, Hill fourth. Patrese, however, is ninth.

As we are constantly reminded, Monaco is all about history and tradition and, while most Grands Prix now start at 2.00, they do not line up here until 3.30. (The other exceptions to the rule are Brazil, 1.00, Italy, 3.00, and Japan, 1.00.) It means you don't have to be up at the crack of dawn and that you may, if you so wish, indulge in a leisurely lunch. Some seek a change of scenery and tempo up in the narrow lanes leading to the Royal Palace. Those who make the laborious climb find it thoroughly rewarding. The sea bass is exquisite today. Others settle for a sandwich and head for the rocks on the other side of the harbour wall to laze for a couple of hours in the sun.

Back at the paddock motorhomes, at the Formula One Paddock Club and at the Yacht Club, the tables are being cleared. The tide of humanity is turning again, making for the pit lane and the hospitality boxes over the pits. With less than an hour to go before the start of the race, the drivers begin to leave their motorhomes, crossing the track at La Rascasse and coming into view for those on the steep hillside. One or two ride up on scooters; most walk. This very public entrance of the gladiators is a rare sight in Formula One. Usually the drivers simply appear from the darkness of their garages, helmets already on. Here, they are followed, cheered or jeered all the way round the sweep into the pit lane and down to their teams. It is yet another example of how Monaco serves to bring the drivers closer to the fans and foster a greater sense of theatre.

Schumacher appears at 2.40, raising whoops from the German contingent. He waves back, a huge grin on his face. Patrese ambles up a few minutes later, the top half of his race-suit down by his waist. He, too, shows his appreciation of the warm applause. The French have their opportunity to exercise their vocal chords when Prost, in white peaked cap, patters beneath them. Last on stage, his blue cap now visible from the midst of photographers and TV crews, is Senna, to a noisy and mixed reception. Apparently undaunted by the whistles, he smiles and waves to the gallery. It seems there can be no middle ground with Senna. Either they love him

Schumacher's hopes are reduced to dust

or they hate him. What no one can dispute is his record here – five wins, including four from the four preceding years. Another victory today would take him past the landmark established by Graham Hill – father of Damon – 24 years ago.

The first corner could be crucial. That can always be the case, of course, but here, where overtaking is so difficult, it might prove decisive. They are all aware of that, none more so than Prost. He has Schumacher and Senna, two recognised chargers, right behind him. The Frenchman must figure that if he can defend his advantage through Ste Devote, he ought to be able to keep the Williams in front.

They are poised on the grid, the longest weekend of the Grand Prix season at last reaching its climax. The red lights are on, then, quite clearly, Prost's car moves forward before they change to green. The rest pursue him round the right-hander and up the hill, leaving the stewards to consider whether the Frenchman had a flyer. The leading drivers hold station through the opening laps, but gradually Schumacher begins to pull away from Senna and turns the heat on Prost.

Seven laps into the race and we hear that Prost has a 10-second stop-and-go penalty for jumping the start. He comes in at the end of the 11th lap and, struggling with a clutch problem, twice stalls. He disconsolately slides out on to the track again more than a lap down on the new leader – Michael Schumacher. The German seizes the initiative and opens a gap of 19 seconds between himself and Senna. That comes down to 13.3 seconds as he has to negotiate backmarkers, and

instantly goes back out to 15 seconds as he eats up a clear lap. Michael is in stunning form, exploring, as he explains, new limits here, leaning into the unforgiving barriers yet never pushing the car that critical centimetre too far. His pace is consistent, his judgment perfect. A race winner in his first full season, he now contemplates victory at Monaco. On the pit wall, the Benetton crew contemplate it, too. At the same time, they are conscious that there is a long, long way to go. This is a 78-lap race, of almost two hours' duration. Anything can happen.

On the 33rd lap, something does happen. Something catastrophic. Schumacher has a problem and eventually rolls to a smoking halt at Loews Hairpin. Marshals smother his stricken B193B in foam and Michael walks away, wringing his hands in despair. Back in the camp, sympathetic pats on the back are scant consolation. Michael is distraught.

'The hydraulic pressure dropped away and I was unable to change gear,' he explains. 'I think it was a failure on the active suspension. To be in the lead, and pulling away, at Monte Carlo is a wonderful sensation. Unfortunately, it did not last long enough.'

It does not last long enough for Patrese, either. He is running sixth, following a tyre change, when his engine fails him and he retires at Mirabeau on the 54th lap. He says: 'There was very little warning. Going through Casino Square I felt something was wrong, and by the time I got to Mirabeau the rear wheels had locked and that was it.'

Senna goes on to claim his record sixth win in the Monaco Grand Prix, fittingly, immediately ahead of Damon Hill. 'If my father was around now he would be the first to congratulate Ayrton,' declares Hill graciously. Michael also has generous words for the man back on top of the World Championship: 'What Ayrton has achieved here is not just exceptional, it is sensational.'

As Senna celebrates, Schumacher restores a positive picture of Benetton's weekend. 'I felt comfortable running at the pace of the Williams and ahead of McLaren,' he concludes. 'I know inside me that we have achieved more this weekend than at any other race this season. Riccardo's retirement was also a blow, but I am sure he will feel the same as I do, once he considers the overall performance of the team during the three working days. Now we know that we will be competitive.'

CHAPTER 9

THE PRESSURE GAME

The Formula One scene switches across the Atlantic, via the obligatory round of tests, to Canada, yet still much of the language and flavour is French. Montreal is, in fact, a cosmopolitan city, the mix creating a vibrant environment and popular destination for the teams. It becomes a little too vibrant on the Wednesday evening before the race. An outbreak of looting and vandalism following Montreal Canadiens' victory over the Los Angeles Kings to secure ice hockey's treasured Stanley Cup. Thousands spill into the downtown streets to celebrate, but the occasion is soured as cars are overturned and shop windows smashed. Stunned visitors leaving restaurants and clubs are confronted with what many describe as being 'like a war zone'.

Tranquillity is at hand. Out on an island in the St Lawrence, a beautiful array of wild flowers is in bloom and ground hogs quietly go about their daily business. Ile Notre Dame consists of fingers of land reaching into the river and the Seaway; within their grasp are the Olympic rowing facility and a lake. Here you will find the Circuit Gilles Villeneuve, home of the Canadian Grand Prix, and on the Thursday the regular pit and paddock routine is under way. The cars and equipment, brought in by air, are unpacked, and the teams' caravans and buses have been parked in place. The setting is pleasant, the track generally regarded as a good test of driving ability and car durability.

Back in the city, Ford are hosting a press conference. In the absence of a Grand Prix in the United States, this is the closest the World Championship comes to home for the company. The defunct Detroit event was right on the doorstep and this weekend, ironically, the IndyCar series stops off in Motown. Here in Montreal, Ford's Formula One drivers are seated in line, ready for introduction. We have Christian Fittipaldi and Fabrizio Barbazza, from Minardi, Johnny Herbert and Alessandro Zanardi, from Lotus, Michael Andretti representing McLaren (Ayrton Senna is a significant absentee), and the Camel Benetton pair, Michael Schumacher and Riccardo Patrese.

Patrese knows it's his turn to stand and say a few words when he hears the preamble include reference to the 'veteran' of Formula One. He seems less amused than his young team-mate, who can scarcely contain himself. Riccardo says that while he has his enthusiasm for the sport, he will go on. FISA having declared their intention to go ahead with the proposed changes to technical regulations for 1994, which will mean the banning of driver aids, Riccardo is asked what effect the decision will have. He replies: 'I think maybe there will be a little more enjoyment in the paddock. Now you are in front of a computer from seven in the morning until eight in the evening. You have not time for human relationships. The show won't suffer and from my point of view I have to say I would like to see it.'

Schumacher is invited to return to the subject of traction control. Yes, he has it here... it was a big step in Monaco... before then they were fighting like crazy but couldn't get the car to the front as they wanted to... this is a driver circuit and he believes traction control will work well here... the team's expectations can get higher from now on.

The formal proceedings over, Michael, tanned and relaxed after a break in the Bahamas and at Disney World, steps down into the gathering and talks at length about the team, himself, his partner and other drivers. First of all, what precisely was the cause of that breakdown in Monaco? He smiles, shakes his head gently, and says: 'Just a small thing that costs almost nothing, an O ring. We were upset, but when you are trying so many things, as we are, this can happen. We are doing in half a year what other teams have done in two or three years. I am still really happy about our performance in Monaco. I was able to keep with Prost, we did a good job and hopefully it will be the same here. I don't expect us to win but we can be second and maybe more.'

Michael's name has been linked with Williams for next season, so how does he react to that and what is his position with Benetton? Again, the smile. 'Last year at Spa, I was already in a McLaren; before that I was sitting in a Ferrari, now in a Williams. The only thing I can say is that it's nice to hear these things because that shows how much potential I have as a driver. But I have a fixed contract with Benetton and that will work for sure next year and maybe the year after – unless Flavio doesn't want me to drive his car!

Schumacher and Patrese check out practice times

'I'm happy, I like the team. They work with me, I work with them. It's a family situation and I think together we are quite strong. We know what we have for each other and there is no need to change anything. Continuity is important. If we go on working together, I don't see why we can't eventually become world champions. I was expecting more of myself and the team this season but now we are coming to a normal situation, and we can still make improvements. Riccardo is doing a good job and if you take away the many problems and bad luck he has had, I think you can see that. I have been able to continue with practice while he has not, that's why I have been in front.'

Michael is asked to consider the plight of Damon Hill, trying to establish himself at Williams. He says: 'I think he will progress with every race, as I did last year. You get more experience and more confidence. At Kyalami, for instance, everything was a bit too much for him and I can understand the situation of being in that car, and having all the expectation to be first or second. It's quite a lot of pressure in your first real season. Damon is a good driver and he is doing a good job. If he has some problems I have a chance to beat him, but he can do an even better job. I have to say, I hope he does have more problems. That will help me.

'I am in only my second season and I have found it is not so much the driving that is a problem for a new driver as the knowledge of Formula One. You have the technical side to learn and you need the overview. The driving is not it. I always give 100 per cent. I have to say I want to drive with traction control now that I have it. Of course, real drivers should say it is better without these things and that driving abil-.ity should be more important, but I am sure some would like to stay with traction control.'

The mechanics could do with the nautical equivalent of traction control as they take to the water for their annual boat race. 'Boat' is a very loose term in the context of this event. Too loose, in some cases. The bizarre contraptions are made from barrels, bottles, tubing and various other paraphernalia strapped together. The furious paddling, splashing and, in some cases, wading ends in victory for the Jordan boys. Goodyear are second and Camel Benetton a heroic third.

■ ■ ■

Friday 11 June, first practice day, dawns wet and cool. The weather here is notoriously erratic. Expect anything is the best tip. Come 9.30, the track is still damp, the skies are still heavy, but at least it is not raining. The odd spin occurs and the appearance of a ground hog on the track surprises no one. Mid-way through the free practice session, however, many are surprised – and angry. Senna's McLaren coasts to a halt on the grass at the Hairpin, out comes the red flag and the car is taken back to the pits. With no spare car allowed, the Brazilian might have been left spectating for the rest of the morning. Instead, his team are able to sort out the electrical problem and put him back to work.

Benetton are among those who feel the action of the officials is unjustified, that the session should not have been stopped and the McLaren should not have been recovered because, they contend, it was not in a dangerous position. Flavio Briatore and team principals of Williams, Ferrari and Minardi register their disapproval with the stewards. Frank Williams reports: 'They said Senna's car was in a dangerous place but we didn't agree and told them what we felt. There was a lot of shouting. It was not very pleasant. This is the second time it's happened in three weeks.'

By the end of the session, and the day, however, Williams are out in front – immediately ahead of Camel Benetton Ford. Schumacher and Patrese maintain the momentum of Monaco with third and fourth places respectively in qualifying. Senna is down in eighth place. Schumacher says: 'Another good performance from us. Apart from a slight gearbox problem, my first run this afternoon was fine. Oil on the track meant I was not able to improve my time. Hopefully it will be our turn for a good result on Sunday.'

Patrese, just a tenth of a second down on his team-mate, is equally content: 'I had a small gearbox problem also, which I didn't have this morning, but it was not too bad. My first run was good and I managed to improve on my second set, despite the oil at the last corner. Without the oil I'm sure I could have improved my time a little more.'

■   ■   ■

You sense that expectations in the camp are rising again. No one is satisfied with results so far, yet now there are clear signs of competitiveness and consistency. The early frustrations have intensified the pressure and made life difficult for everyone, not least those specifically involved in creating the car. If the designers and engineers don't produce the goods, no amount of driving talent can deliver.

Ross Brawn maintains that McLaren's form at the start of the season did not catch him off guard. 'I expected them to be pretty strong,' he says. 'Where we fell down slightly was in having a lot of new stuff, so we weren't quite on top of it for the beginning of the season. We knew the new car would be worth a reasonable amount on performance and we just wanted to get it out for Donington. In the last few races we've started to get on top of

the new car and we're doing the job. Where we're at now is at least where I expected us to be and we still need to go a bit further to challenge Williams.'

Has there been any regret that so many steps were taken with the car for this year? 'I think there are two points of view: either that you are taking on too much but you knuckle down and sort it out; or you get half-way through the season and wish you'd put the gearbox on or done the active suspension. You are then powerless to do anything, whereas with the first situation you just dig a bit deeper and sort out the problems. You've got all the kit on the car and although you may have to go on for a race or two with that situation, you know you have the means to go forward, and that's my philosophy on it.

'There is a lot of pressure on me and the rest of the team. It is very much a team effort, involving Rory Byrne, Pat Symonds, Frank Dernie and many others. I think we all feel the pressure performing, particularly when we've got good drivers. Riccardo seems to be coming to terms with the way we operate and the way the car works. Michael is very quick. So there are no excuses and there's always a lot of pressure on. You're tested every two weeks. There's an evaluation of what sort of job you are doing. Success is due to many people but in a way failure is down to me, because if a group of engineers aren't producing the goods then that's my responsibility, so I feel some direct pressure, for sure.'

For all the pressures, Brawn somehow manages to sustain an unruffled demeanour. 'I tend to try and keep quiet to get things done,' he says. 'I don't know whether it's constructive to lose your rag. That does happen occasionally, but it tends to be behind closed doors. I think that's the only way to operate. It's a bit melodramatic to start screaming and shouting in the pit lane. Not my style.'

Ross Brawn

Apart from a five-year period with the Atomic Energy Research Establishment at Harwell, Brawn's working life has been devoted to motor racing. He had eight years at Williams, gathering knowledge in every aspect of the design and production of a Formula One car, before joining the ill-fated FORCE team venture as chief aerodynamicist. After that brief episode he became Arrows' chief designer and then linked up with Tom Walkinshaw at TWR, where he designed the Sportscar World Championship-winning Jaguar XJR-14. Walkinshaw duly brought him back into Grand Prix racing.

Brawn, 39, has found his release from the pressures of the job in fishing, more recently gardening, and in family life. He is married, with two daughters. 'In the last few years I've got into gardening in a big way,' he says. 'It's strange. My old man had been involved in gardening for years and I could never see the attraction, but now I've found it to be such a good diversion and form of relaxation. I've bought a house with a three-acre garden. It used to be lovely and on a list of exceptional gardens in the area, but unfortunately the lady owner grew ill and old, and it deteriorated. It's my ambition to put it back to how it was.

'It gives me a bit of physical exercise and once I get involved in it I generally clear my head of what's happening in racing, and I think that's essential. It depends on the individual. We've got one or two people in the team who don't need the release. I do. I need to have something else and I think it makes me better for it. So I can perhaps have a weekend off and come in on a Monday morning fully charged up, ready to go and tackle it.

'My wife is very keen on the garden and all the family are very interested in the racing. They do feel the ups and downs. The younger one, who's 11, takes it all to heart. But they have also learned that when I come home I don't want to discuss it. I like to forget about work. After a heavy day or week I need to switch off and fortunately they can read me well enough not to ask why Michael didn't finish at Monaco or whatever.'

Soon Brawn and his colleagues must begin work on next year's car, their task complicated by the on-going uncertainty over technical regulations, even though FISA have declared that driver aids will be banned from next season. 'The problem lands on the engineer's plate,' he says. 'The decisions themselves aren't perhaps as important as the right timing for them. The fact that the thing has been debated so much means we don't have a clear picture of what's going to happen.

'I think the brief that's been given by FISA is pretty ambiguous. I know they say they'll answer any questions to clarify the situation, but I think they should be defining what they want us to do because it is inherent in Formula One that you take advantage of the regulations to the maximum. For instance, what is active suspension? If somebody could properly define it, perhaps they could say they are not going to allow it. I think the FISA quote is "anything that changes the trim of the car automatically". Well, what exactly is that?

'I can see it being a very contentious issue at the beginning of the season. You've got to make decisions on how you are going to conduct your programme. Are you going to accept the regulation in what could be described as "the true spirit" – and not much of that exists in Formula One – or will you take it to the limit because you don't want to be outdone by another major team who come in with a broader interpretation of the regulation? I hope FISA are not using the looseness of the description of active suspension to enable them to take whatever interpretation they choose, because that would just end in tears. You'll turn up at a track and someone will decree that your interpretation is incorrect. It's a can of worms.

'It's the fact that it's not clear that's the biggest frustration. We've been talking about next year's car for several months now. We have to start committing ourselves, with drawings or manufacturing information, in August, so it's not long before we've got to make a decision on what we're going to do next year and stick to it. If we start changing direction it's really going to be costly in terms of performance, reliability and so on.'

Ross still has unfulfilled aspirations for this season. 'We've got to start winning some races,' he says. 'Monaco was very unfortunate but at least we were there. I think we'll be competitive here in the race. Winning a few races is the least of what we should be aiming to achieve. Certainly we need to try to finish second in the Championship. Williams should be running away with it by now, but for various reasons they are not. We've got to improve our act and aim to finish second. So we've still got a lot of ambition for the rest of the season.'

By Saturday, the saga of the regulations has moved on apace. A document, issued by the stewards of the meeting but instigated by FISA, indicates that every team except Lola Ferrari have illegal cars and they must be changed. The edict refers to moving parts and systems not under the control of the driver – in other words, active suspension and traction control. Disbelief, rather than anger, appears to envelop the pit lane. The general message from the teams is that they cannot and will not strip their cars of active suspension before the French Grand Prix on 4 July.

Brawn says: 'We couldn't do it within a couple of weeks. Really, it would take six months because the car is designed as an active car, aerodynamically and mechanically. To get it back to being a passive car is a six-month project. It would also incur a lot of cost to go back to a passive car this year. Active cars have been running for seven or eight years, so why have they chosen this time to reinforce the interpretation of the regulation? This actually means that we won the Championship last year because the cars that beat us were illegal. Interesting point. I think their interpretation is a bit cavalier, so I see this as a bit of sabre-rattling.'

■ ■ ■

There is a real battle to be fought out on the Circuit Gilles Villeneuve. The uncertainty of yesterday's weather has given way to the certainty of a hot second practice day. The sky is blue, the sun is bright. Patrese becomes a little blue, too. He says: 'At the beginning of my second run in qualifying the engine stopped. It happened on the final straight, right in front of Prost. I hope I didn't cause any problems for him.'

Jim Brett, of Cosworth Engineering, admits: 'We were trying something different on the final run with Riccardo's car, but unfortunately it didn't pay off.'

Patrese is also fortunate that the hot conditions have made the track slower. The top eight drivers are unable to improve their times and their positions on the grid remain unchanged. Patrese will start the race from fourth place, Schumacher from third.

Michael has had a smoother run. 'Another fantastic day,' he enthuses. 'We made some changes for qualifying and all went well. I almost equalled my time from yesterday, which is not too bad considering the hotter conditions today. We can feel optimistic for the race. The gearbox problem from yesterday is cured and I feel even more confident with the car.'

And what about the knee? 'I have been doing a lot of special exercises to overcome the problems and it is feeling a lot better. I had too much friction in the joint and I am told I will need at least a three-week break if I have surgery. I do a lot of stretching and we shall have to wait and see in the winter if I need an operation.'

■ ■ ■

Race day, too, is hot and sunny. Schumacher increases the temperature at the front by splitting the Williams cars in warm-up. Patrese is eighth but apparently has no problems. There's a buzz in the Camel Benetton Ford compound, a spring in the step of team personnel. Those who can, take a lunch-time break beneath umbrellas, mingling with guests. Pasta, chatter and optimism are the order of the day; Flavio Briatore likes that. He is not so keen on the prospect of another conflict over regulation changes, suggestions of his interest in acquiring Renault engines, or anything he considers negative and detrimental to the show. Parking himself on a large blue crate, he presents his case for fuel stops, fewer mechanics at pit stops – and more women in the paddock.

'Here we are again,' he says, 'with more rumour, rumour, rumour, bad headlines, nobody talking about the race, the show. We have to think more about the public and the sponsors and give them what they want. Now a car comes in, you can't see it for mechanics, and it's out again in a few seconds. Sponsors don't see their names and you don't get enough changes of the leading positions. The way it is going, you might as well have a computerised pit stop in the garage and no one would see anything at all. Is that what you want? No, we want to make the show better, make it cheaper and more fun. We want girls around here, not all these boring men – and that includes me.'

Steve Parker

Benetton do, in fact, have a mixed party of guests. Some are with Ford, here represented in strength. Steve Parker, Ford's Formula One boss, helps himself to a coffee and smartly steps away from the cheese board. 'This race is near to home but it's a shame there's not a US Grand Prix,' he says. 'We've got pole in the IndyCar race at Detroit, which is great news. It's just a pity for racegoers that they conflict. It would be sad to have a war between IndyCars and Formula One because I would have thought there was room for both series alongside one another. Maybe in the long term the thing would be to try and merge into one formula and operate on both continents. It would certainly be attractive from Ford's point of view.'

What is Ford's view on the stories linking Benetton with Renault? Parker is philosophical: 'I think if I was in the business of running a racing team I would certainly want to keep my options open and be mindful of what opportunities were available. I'd be talking to other manufacturers, seeing what's happening on the engine scene, what developments there are, and I would expect them to be doing that.

'There are a number of things that Ford get out of Formula One. The easy one is publicity. I'm actually a marketing person. It's an enormous sport. There are 400 million people watching each event on television, which puts Formula One next to the World Cup and the Olympics. There are up to 300,000 people who physically travel to watch the events. So that's why you see so many brand names on the cars. It's very powerful.

'More interesting, though, from a motor manufacturer's point of view, are the other benefits we can get out of it. One of them is an *esprit de corps*. It is very important to have your work force motivated and that's a very difficult thing to manage when you're talking about hundreds of thousands of employees. We publicise our activities in Formula One vigorously internally and we have an enormously strong following. There will be a terrific number of Ford people watching this race, saying, "go on, win it, do it". That's very good.

'We've also got a very strong engineering involvement and that's really with our electronics division. We have around 20 engineers dedicated to Formula One, working at it full time, and a number of other engineers are adding peripheral support. There are two reasons for that: one is that there is a lot of feedback coming out of the electronics side into the car industry – things like active ride, for instance. We are quite confident we will be putting active ride on to a production car within the next three years or so. All the development done on that will be directly useful to us. It's work we would have had to do anyway.

'Active is one of the targets in the rule changes, which is a bit of a shame. That's one of the downs. I think it's understandable. You've got people whose whole aspirations in life are dedicated, totally focused on winning, and when you get 10 or 12 people in one room it's not easy to reach agreements. Fortunately, in the work we've already done, working with Benetton, developing active and putting it on their car, we have done most of the groundwork already. I would like to have seen it saved for another year because I think we would have found some more refinements on it, but at least it's not come at an absolutely disastrous time for us.

'I don't know the IndyCar scene but from what I hear they don't seem to have all the confrontations we see in Formula One. The IndyCar series appears to be run more smoothly. There are some lessons Formula One could learn from IndyCars, I'm sure of that.'

■   ■   ■

The drivers have to share the pre-race limelight with the local sporting heroes, the Canadiens, here to show off the Stanley Cup (a huge, grotesque trophy) and lap up the applause of the gallery. No riots or overturned cars this time.

Once the Grand Prix cars are in place on the grid, most of the drivers climb out and try to stay cool and relaxed. Schumacher shares a joke with his engineers. Patrese looks a little more serious. Both amble around their cars. And then it's time to go. They complete the formation lap and steady themselves, Michael behind Prost, Riccardo behind Hill.

The Williams pair get away but the Benettons are swallowed up by Senna's McLaren and the Ferraris of Berger and Alesi. At the end of the first lap Patrese is sixth, Schumacher seventh. Michael says: 'I felt I might have had a chance to overtake at least one of the Williams at the start but it all went terribly wrong. We had a problem with the traction control adjustment and twice I nearly stalled. We will change the setting for the next race.'

The pressure is on, and Schumacher seems to revel in it. On the second lap he takes his team-mate for sixth place, on the third he passes Alesi for fifth and on the sixth he has Berger for fourth. Patrese has a wall of red Ferrari in front of him; first Alesi, then Berger. They are embroiled in a tense tussle.

A breakdown in communications at Williams costs Hill a lengthy pit stop and he slips down to fourth, behind Senna and Schumacher, who rises to the challenge of tracking down the Brazilian. Patrese's hopes are deflated when he spins, breaking off part of the front wing, and comes into the pits for repairs. Nine laps later he is back in the pits for good. He explains: 'I was having cramp in my right leg and it got worse. In the end I could not feel the leg at all. I could not carry on.'

Schumacher is not only carrying on, he is reeling in Senna. The two men are trading fastest laps, but the German is getting the better of the deal. A five-second gap after the pit stops is down to 1.5 seconds after 58 laps. Eleven laps remain. Next time round the gap is 0.9 seconds; after 61 laps it's 0.5. On the 63rd lap Schumacher is preparing to attack when suddenly the McLaren slows and appears to veer to the right. Both cars twitch and the Benetton just squeezes through on the outside. Senna cruises to a standstill with an alternator failure. Michael follows in Prost to take second place, ahead of Hill.

'I like a good fight and I enjoyed my battle with Senna,' says Schumacher, 'but perhaps it was a little too close on this occasion. I was lucky to get through and lucky not to hit the wall. Maybe he didn't see me. He appeared to slow down as I was catching, so maybe he was just tired and wanted to stop for a rest!'

Michael is enjoying himself all right, and throws himself into the spirit of the podium ceremony. 'Things have gone so well I just feel very happy and I like being up there with that champagne. It is what racing is all about. Coming back from seventh to second is almost as good as a win for us.' He is still smiling as he strides from the circuit. Riccardo is a few paces behind. His solemn face tells its own story.

Champagne Schumacher

Flavio, heading for the airport, rues the 'bad starts' and wonders aloud what might have been. He meets his former driver Martin Brundle, who finished fifth in the Ligier. 'Schuey drove well,' says the Englishman. 'He did a 24.8 straight from the pit stop. That's impressive. Most do about a 27. Schuey just continues where he left off. Yeah, that's impressive.'

Flavio nods. 'Mm.'

CHAPTER 10

TALKING HEADS

That faulty start in Montreal is still on the minds of Camel Benetton Ford and, more importantly, on the agenda when the team head for the pre-British Grand Prix test at Silverstone. The general sense of progress is invigorating. Another piece of the jigsaw needs to be slightly reshaped, that's all. So much of the picture is clear now and that provides the spur to complete it. Michael Schumacher, armed with adjusted traction control, practises starts, blasting the B193B down the Northamptonshire tarmac. It looks, and sounds, hugely impressive.

One or two engine problems appear less to the liking of Benetton, Ford and Cosworth, though by the end of the three-day session the times are reasonably

Stage fright... singer Paul Young seems to be having second thoughts about a spin in Schumacher's Mondeo

encouraging. Schumacher, joined here by Riccardo Patrese and one of the team's test drivers, Andrea Montermini, splits the Williams pair, Damon Hill and Alain Prost.

Schumacher also amuses himself at the wheel of a Ford Mondeo saloon, entertaining (if that is the word) journalists to a ride around the circuit. It has always been my belief that racing drivers relish this opportunity to exact some sort of sadistic revenge for literary maltreatment, actual or (more usually) imagined, in the past. It may matter not that the scribe strapped in the seat alongside has never even written about the driver before, let alone wronged him; this is a crusade against a profession. Michael, as ever, is good value, and provides a glimpse of the judgment and car control that set the professionals apart from the dreamers.

■ ■ ■

Not for the first time this season, the Benetton team are the focus of much attention and conjecture when they arrive at Magny-Cours for the French Grand Prix. It is known that RJ Reynolds International Inc. have for some time been considering their future in Formula One, and on the morning of Friday 2 July, they announce they will not be renewing their sponsorship in 1994. Camel has been the title sponsor of Benetton Ford and a major backer of Williams since 1991. The corporation headquarters are in the United States but the heartbeat of the Formula One sponsorship is a British-based company called Global Event Management, a sports marketing subsidiary of RJR Nabisco. Its managing director is Duncan Lee, the Formula One sponsorship manager Richard Grundy. Their dejection over the decision is apparent and understandable.

In the seclusion of the Camel motorhome, Grundy says: 'Camel came into Formula One at the beginning of 1987 as part of a strategy to build the brand into a global name. It had been decided to prioritise three of the many brands Reynolds owned, those three being Camel, Winston and Salem, a menthol cigarette. The vehicle chosen for Camel was Formula One, which is a global sport with a worldwide following and TV audiences of billions. When a sponsor arrives on the scene here it's as if you are a newcomer to a little village. Formula One is a community, moving from place to place like a travelling circus. A newcomer in any community needs time to be accepted. It takes time for people to get to know you. People who are already there want to know if you are a serious player, if you're there for the long haul. We felt we weren't truly accepted until about our fourth or fifth year. Bernie Ecclestone made a comment at the end of the '91 season on the lines of "we can do this for you and that for you because you're family" and we felt then that we'd been accepted. We'd paid our dues.

'It would be indiscreet of me to give exact figures on what we have put into Formula One but the cumulative investment since '87 is substantial; over 100 million dollars, let's say that. You've got to bear in mind that a lot of traditional forms of advertising are closed off for cigarette brands due to legal restraints that operate now in many countries. Sponsorship is what they call "below the line" advertising, as opposed to "above the line" advertising, such as you might see on television or billboards. Television advertising is banned almost universally now, so the big plus for sponsorship, particularly of Formula One, is that you can get global television exposure, which isn't otherwise possible. It's one of the few vehicles which enables you to do that.

'From this vehicle you generate marketing spin-offs. You can use Formula One as a basis for local promotions, you can use it for

Wired for the sound of Benetton at work

sales promotion in stores where the product is sold, you can use it at airport shops, you can use it as a PR tool and in some places you can feature Formula One sponsorship in your advertising. It can be used as a basis for prizes and trade hospitality. It also engenders good morale within the company, a factor often under-estimated. It is something everybody follows. It's good for team spirit, it brings people together and gives them a common cause.

'It's very hard to quantify the success of a "below the line" activity such as this. There are any number of market research companies which would claim to be able to give you accurate data which directly equate sponsorship with an increase in sales. You've got to see sponsorship as part of your overall marketing mix. It's just one strand in a strategy to promote your product and the cumulative effect of sponsorships, of promotions in the field, of such advertising that you can do, is to create an image and to raise the brand's profile. All the different strands are working towards the same goal and over time the cumulative effect is to lift the sales graph.

'Camel, until very recently, had been growing at quite a steady rate in terms of sales. It is not at the moment and I expect that goes for all tobacco makers. They are all having a hard time. A notable chunk of our business was in the Middle East and it's no longer possible to do business there for political reasons.

'If you are a big sponsor in Formula One you need to be identified as a player rather than just a name on the side of a car. That's why we took on a public relations company, Jardine PR. Tony Jardine comes to most of the races and Maria Bellanca, who is employed by him and works as our press officer, comes to all the races. They handle a PR programme for us. It consists of many things but basically it's a news and information service for which we have a mailing list, a distribution list which runs into many thousands around the world, providing information for Camel markets and media. In tandem with that we also have a photographic service, provided by a photographer contracted to Jardine PR.

Richard Grundy

'While Jardine PR handle automotive and sporting media, Patrizia Spinelli is the press officer for Benetton and her brief is to look after lifestyle publications – the glossies, publications which normally would not show an interest in Formula One but are interested because Benetton is a fashion name. Ford, of course, have their own PR people and Sophie Sicot is their press officer here. It all fits together quite nicely.

'We liaise all the time with Benetton. It's an on-going dialogue. We talk every day on a range of issues, not just marketing and public relations but small things too: how the clothes should be embroidered, where the stickers should go on the car. New sponsors, smaller ones, come and go, and all these things have to be accommodated to the satisfaction of the title sponsor, and that's where I fit in. If they need any input from me, if they have questions on what is acceptable to Camel, then they pick up the phone and talk to me.

'The decision to withdraw from Formula One sponsorship was taken at the very highest level of the corporation. The rationale is that Camel has had a very fruitful association with Formula One, we know that it is a proven and effective marketing tool, not just for us but for any global name. However, it has been decided there are now other priorities and that what was good when we came in, in '87, and has been good up to '93, is no longer the case. We have to find other things for Camel, pursue other directions. The priorities for our business have been altered in the last few weeks. There's a new business plan and this decision has been taken in accordance with that business plan.

'It is a big disappointment to me personally and to Duncan, my boss. He was there right from the start. I came in '89. We've come a long way. In the first three years we were learning. We sponsored Lotus, which was initially extremely suc-

cessful but once Senna had gone it became apparent he had been carrying the team. They started on a slow decline which accelerated towards the end of our association, which was at the end of '90, and we realised that with the kind of money we were spending we had to be with top teams to get a return on our investment.

'You've got to be with teams that are capable of finishing in the first three and getting drivers on the podium. That means understanding that a team has to have certain things: a works engine, top line drivers, focused management and so on. That's the sort of thing we learnt at the time. If you want to promote positive image values, you've got to be with the top teams. If you're with teams at the back of the grid you are not achieving that. In fact, it's almost counter-productive.

'We had a good year in '91 with Mansell challenging for the Championship at Williams. In '92, Mansell and Williams won the titles and we dominated the podium. Benetton scored points in every single race. We had a lot of exposure and really showed our main competitors, Marlboro, the way to go. It's a similar story this season. The last three years have paid back in a big way. It's a shame we are not going to be around to maximise the success we've now got.

'It's not by accident that we are in this dominant position. To finally figure out how it all works and to get there, to achieve success and then to walk away is frustrating. We built this programme into something big and something very successful, we have a very good image now both inside and outside the sport, and it is personally sad for Duncan and myself – we've both put in a lot of good work. I don't think it would have made any difference if we had come to an agreement with Williams. The decision from the corporation would still have been that we withdraw from Formula One as a consequence of those changed business priorities I mentioned earlier. To be perfectly honest, I do not know what those changed priorities are. It seems to me there is no focused strategy for this particular brand. Cutting Formula One is to deprive Camel of its main international vehicle.

'I actually came to an agreement with Flavio Briatore at the Monaco Grand Prix this year that, come what may with Camel, I would leave GEM at the end of the year to take up a position as Marketing Director at Benetton, working directly for Flavio. As a consequence of what has now happened, that date has been moved forward and I shall be starting after the British Grand Prix. The job will involve running the marketing department, controlling the public relations for the team, servicing existing sponsors and looking for new ones. The most pressing priority is to replace Camel. We've got to find a sponsor to fill the hole and that's not going to be easy.

'I have first-hand experience of what the team is like. I've had to deal with them every working day for the last three years and I feel there have been some shortcomings. The upper management is extremely good and the team is led very well by Flavio and Tom. But on the marketing side there is a management vacuum, if you like, in the middle. Below Flavio there's no-one there with sufficient experience to know how to deal with a major corporation, who knows what the objectives are, and who really understands what a big brand such as Camel is aiming to achieve through an F1 sponsorship.

'I've found that frustrating at times as I've been held responsible for things that did or did not happen due to shortcomings on the Benetton side. I've often protested my innocence by saying I work for Camel, I don't work for Benetton. I can't do their job too! There were a couple of instances over the winter of '91 where I was really taken to task, justifiably and understandably, but I took these points to Flavio. I told him I was getting it in the neck and it wasn't all my fault and that if he wanted to retain sponsors long-term he needed to rectify these things. I think he took those points on board and I'm flattered that he's hired me to do the job.

'It's nice to go into an environment you already know. I know a lot of guys on the team, I know Flavio extremely well. So I know roughly what to expect and it's nice to be forearmed. Not everyone has that advantage going into a new job. The priority, then, is to find new investors and, once we've got them, we intend running a one-stop exploitation package for them. That's going to take a lot of work. We want to set up for them the PR, co-ordinate their exploitation programmes, and organise a complete service package which enables them to maximise their involvement with the team to the fullest effect. The idea is to keep them

Max Mosley and Flavio Briatore

as long-term partners. That's good for their business and for ours as well, of course, as it brings stability to the team, which in turn will help its competitiveness on the track; and that will keep it attractive to sponsors. That's how it all works.'

Flavio, true to character, puts a brave face on developments. Holding court in the middle of the paddock, he smiles and gestures in a way that renders the words unnecessary. He says it anyway: 'No worries. It's now July, 1993. It's a long time to 1994. I think we shall have something to announce long before then. Maybe in a few weeks.'

Word of the announcement spreads through the garages like a bush fire. The boys at Benetton see the prospect of some consolation. They will have extra stock at the end-of-season sale, when mechanics traditionally pocket what they can from punters in Adelaide, eager to get their hands on genuine Grand Prix racing-team gear. Camel Benetton Ford shirts and accessories have suddenly assumed the status of collectors' items.

Words are in full flow this weekend. Following the edict at Montreal, FISA now say they will hold an extraordinary World Council meeting in Paris, on 15 and 16 July, to consider reports of alleged technical and fuel irregularities. Max Mosley, president of FISA, takes the opportunity here to 'clarify' the situation, admitting it was felt there was no alternative but to wield the big stick and that action had been decided on after threats of legal proceedings from some quarters. Teams were warned that points could be deducted but Mosley insists that any decisions will be 'fair and reasonable'.

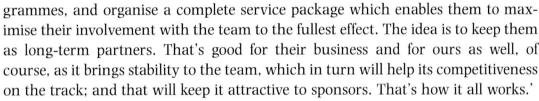

Action on the track comes as a massive relief to everyone. The sun eventually breaks down a stubborn early morning cloud cover and a hot afternoon is in prospect. The pace of the B193B is not quite what Schumacher, Patrese and their engineers would have liked. Only French teams have been allowed to test here prior to the meeting so, for Benetton and the majority of teams, this weekend is a scramble to find an ideal – or at least adequate – set-up. By the end of the first qualifying session the temperature is such that the lap times are slower, but Michael has third place in the bag. Riccardo can manage only 11th.

Schumacher says: 'After this morning's practice I really didn't expect to be in a position to set third fastest time in qualifying. Nothing seemed to be working and we weren't making much progress, but obviously the changes we made during the break worked well. I'm still not sure what the trouble was in the morning but I was much happier this afternoon. The only problem I had was with first gear and that caused me to spin on my last lap.'

Patrese's grim expression has not changed all day. 'Not a very good day for me,' he says, shaking his head. 'We changed the set-up for qualifying but it's still not right. We don't have enough grip and, on top of that, I don't think we chose the right moment to go out this afternoon. Either there was traffic or the track was not at its best. I really hope it doesn't rain tomorrow because there's a lot of potential in the car and we hope to go much better.'

■ ■ ■

It certainly doesn't look like rain on the Saturday. Patches of mist soon succumb to the sun and Patrese will have his chance to improve. 'We couldn't quite get it right yesterday,' concedes Ross Brawn. 'It is such a difficult circuit on which to get it right. Still, it's the same for everybody and we've got another day to get there.'

Words are very much a part of practice and racing, too. Team personnel and drivers communicate by radio, the only means of eavesdropping, a headset. We have the opportunity to listen in on the conversation between drivers and engineers during this second morning's practice, the one-and-a-half-hour session generally regarded as crucial to any team's race preparation. While Wayne Bennett, an electronics technician, sorts out the headsets at the back of the truck, Rory Byrne, currently acting as Patrese's race engineer, checks the temperature of the tyres, stacked in their heaters. Frank Dernie is in charge of Schumacher's car and Brawn oversees the pit operation. Flavio Briatore and Tom Walkinshaw are stationed with other engineers on the pit wall.

Wired for sound, we can now discover what these talking heads are saying. Channel One is Schumacher's, Channel Two Patrese's and Channel Three is to Pit. On Scan, however, we can pick up whatever is coming in and get a more general insight. Scan it is. Schumacher is sitting in his cockpit for the 9.30 start, ready to try the car on a full tank of fuel, about 200 litres. 'I want to make sure everything is okay,' he tells the crew. The German, like his Italian team-mate, communicates in English.

Patrese follows his partner on to the circuit two minutes later and their mechanics have a brief respite. Some lean on the work benches, others simply hover in wait. The crew on the spare car have their hands full with the back end. Schumacher is the first back. He says: 'The car is as near perfect as it was in qualifying yesterday, but still a little nervous.' He goes into a precise analysis of the car's performance on every corner, all of which is logged by attentive engineers.

The drivers are also trying a new drink-bottle system, which will be welcomed in a hot race. Schumacher says: 'The drink is okay, it's just that it does not fall back quickly enough into the bottle.'

Patrese returns and enters into a dialogue about understeer and oversteer with Byrne. Patrese says: 'The automatic change-down is not as quick as I would like.'

Byrne: 'Maybe we can change that for qualifying or warm-up. Riccardo, try a start at the end of the pit lane, then two flying laps.'

9.46 – Schumacher is in the pits again. 'Take 100 litres out of Michael's car,' his crew are instructed. Schumacher says: 'It is better, especially in the high-speed corners. The car is not rolling. It is much more stable. The circuit temperature has increased again and you can feel this.' He climbs from his car and goes into a huddle with his engineers.

9.51 – Patrese is in again. 'The brakes are cooking a little bit,' he says.

Byrne: 'Did you do a start?'

Patrese: 'Yes, a lot of vibration. Do we have another scrubbed set [of tyres]?'

Byrne: 'I'm just a bit nervous about the front left. It's not coming up to pressure.... Michael thought the balance on full tanks was quite good... Riccardo, the next run will be on new tyres, just give us five minutes.'

Brawn calmly enquires: 'Can we have Michael Schumacher in the car?'

Someone comes in: 'Don't know where he is. Think he's been given the day off.'

Schumacher, over by the pit wall, gets the message. He vaults a barrier, heads smartly for the back of the garage and pulls on his helmet. Before driving off, he says: 'We do have a problem with the radio, a big crackle, so I take it off for the run.'

Both drivers are out again, leaving a mechanic to sweep the garage floor. A colleague mischievously tosses down a bottle top but the mechanic carries on regardless. The floor gleams.

10.10 – Schumacher is back, positive as ever: 'Compared to yesterday, it is definitely an improvement. Just a little problem going into fourth gear. The car is much more consistent in high-speed corners. The second lap could have been quicker. I went a bit wide on turn six.'

The reply comes back: 'We saw that on TV.'

There is no hiding place here.

Dernie: 'Can you get out please, Michael? Covers on the tyres, please.'

10.11 – Patrese is in: 'I have a vibration and a problem changing down from fourth to third.'

A Goodyear engineer checks the temperatures of the tyres removed from Patrese's car.

Patrese: 'Can we put the car as Michael's? We should copy their car. Can you look, please, what are the differences?'

Byrne: 'The only difference now is that Michael is running one degree less front wing.'

Brawn: 'I think we should try that, Riccardo, because he's quite happy with that this morning.'

Patrese sits patiently in his car, monitoring the lap times, as technicians tap at their computers. Byrne paces the garage and checks his watch. It's 10.24. Still Byrne paces. He checks his watch again – 10.25.

Schumacher is ready to go again: 'I can't put the radio in because I'll go crazy with it.'

10.20 – Patrese's car is fired up. Byrne: 'This is two flying laps, but if you want a third, okay.'

10.32 – Patrese, entering the pit lane: 'We want to check where the problem is. There is no balance. I can't drive the car like this. The front is not there.'

Patrese's car is pushed back into the garage.

Byrne: 'Wrap the tyres and plug them in.'

Patrese: 'There is a problem. He goes quick, I can't. It is not a question to put back what we had. We must do something to correct the car because I don't think it's right.'

Byrne, Brawn and Patrese

Schumacher, patently more content, is back and sitting on a bench, ringed by engineers.

Byrne: 'I can't see anything visible that's wrong. We'll check after the session. I think we'll have to plug into the original wing settings and ride-height maps.'

Patrese: 'Okay, okay. The problem is that the car is understeering like hell. I can't drive the car and go quick. No way.'

Dernie issues instructions for front-wing adjustments to be made on Schumacher's car.

Frustration is still gnawing at Patrese: 'How can I drive like that, with no front end?'

Byrne, retaining his composure: 'We could give it more front end.'

Patrese, nodding: 'Okay, let's see what happens. I am running short of ideas to give the car balance. It oversteers, it understeers, never something neutral.'

Schumacher goes back to work as Byrne calls for another set of tyres for Patrese.

Byrne: 'You have five laps and you have ten minutes, so use the time. You might as well learn as much as you can.'

Dernie: 'Michael, come in now.'

Schumacher: 'I think that was another step forward, an overall improvement. Maybe we want to continue in this direction in the afternoon.'

Brawn: 'What about the straight-line speed?'

Schumacher: 'I had to overtake Prost once.'

Schumacher's cornering style

Patrese: 'I have a problem with the gearbox at the end of the straight. It didn't want to change down. I'm coming in. I have a problem. It didn't change down to second. It stayed in sixth.'

Patrese rolls into view: 'I'm changing down normally, not using auto. Changing down, it stayed in sixth, or maybe down to fifth.... I don't know if it's somebody else or my car, but there is a big smell of something burning. A bad smell.... The balance has come back a little bit.'

It is 10.54.

Patrese is asked: 'Do you want to get out of the car?'

He does.

The headsets are collected, another practice session over. Schumacher is fourth fastest, Patrese 14th. The overriding impression is that, for all the advance of technology and computer input, there remains no substitute for driver feedback. 'You can't beat the information from the guy with his bum on the seat,' says Gordon Message. 'Yeah, that was a fairly typical session, really.'

Benetton take the calculated risk of going with A tyres (the harder compound) rather than Bs in qualifying, but the temperature is not as high as they anticipated and their opponents achieve more grip. Schumacher will start the race from seventh on the grid, Patrese, who has had a spin, from 12th. Message says: 'In hindsight, I suppose you have to admit it was the wrong way to go, but had it been hotter it might have been very different.'

Schumacher says: 'Sometimes you have to gamble on these occasions and it didn't quite work for us this afternoon. I had a lot of oversteer on my first run. The car was better on the second set but it was not perfect, particularly in the high-speed corners. Seventh on the grid is not what we had hoped for. I'll just have to wait and see what happens in the race. I'll not predict anything because overtaking is quite difficult here, but not impossible.'

Patrese reports: 'Because I lost a lot of time this morning that obviously affected what we were able to do when it came to improving the car for qualifying. We have had a lot of small problems and I have still not found the best balance with the car. I didn't have the opportunity to run with full tanks this morning but Michael did and he said the car was good. We have a lot of thinking to do tonight.'

■　■　■

Race day, 4 July, is hot. It is going to be something of an ordeal for drivers and spectators alike. This is the third French Grand Prix to be held at the Magny-Cours circuit, just south of Nevers, in Burgundy. It is an excellent facility, though a less than inspiring race track. The best overtaking opportunity is to be had at Adelaide Hairpin, where Schumacher and others have had a little excitement in the past.

Despite the experience in final qualifying, Michael, conscious of tyre-wear problems here, elects to race on As. Riccardo decides to take the same course. One other driver, Ferrari's Jean Alesi, goes for As instead of Bs. Riccardo, still dissatisfied with his regular car, opts to race the spare. The pit lane opens at 1.30 and he takes the car round the circuit. He returns, is pushed back into the garage and goes into consultation with engineers. There is feverish activity about the Camel Benetton Ford before he leaves again, ahead of the pit-lane closing, at 1.45. His crew are there to meet him on the grid and pounce on the car again. The grid is cleared, the car's bodywork is replaced and Patrese, like Schumacher, is set to go racing.

Patrese's fortunes scarcely improve, however. He seems constantly hemmed in by traffic and runs up the rear wheels of Christian Fittipaldi's Minardi Ford, losing his front wing and consequently forfeiting more time in the pits. He manages to bustle his way back to 10th at the end.

Schumacher stays out of trouble and runs sixth in the early stages, advancing a place when Ligier's Mark Blundell comes to grief. He emerges fourth from a second flurry of pit stops, immediately behind Senna's McLaren Ford. Ahead of them are the Williams Renault pair, Prost and Hill. 'I made the decision to stop the first time but I was surprised to see the arrow to come in for a second change. We had to try something to catch Senna and it was absolutely the right decision. I compliment the team.'

Senna, who stays with his second set of tyres, is hauled in by the charging Schumacher. Forty-seventh time round, Michael posts the fastest lap. At the end of the 54th lap they are 2.7 seconds

Schumacher shows Hill (left) and Prost how to enjoy success

apart. Two laps later the gap is merely 0.6 seconds. Senna resists and Schumacher bides his time. The moment arrives on lap 64, eight from the end, and the green and yellow car swoops into third place. It is the only overtaking manoeuvre at the front of the field. The crowd have a French winner, Prost, yet little else by way of entertainment. The pre-race parade of drivers in open-top vintage cars was well received, but perhaps the highlight is a dousing from water hoses at the end.

Schumacher is satisfied enough. He says: 'I knew the car would be good for the race and that I would have a good chance to pass Senna, but I could not get close enough coming out of the fast corner. Eventually, though, it came. It was a nice battle again. We couldn't finish it in Canada but we did here and I'm happy to say I won it. Usually he takes advantage of the back markers but today I was able to do so. It was another good result for us.'

Briatore says: 'To finish third behind the two Williams is as good as a win for us. We are more than happy. The team's strategy was very good. The tyre changes were excellent. After a difficult start to our weekend, third place is the very best we could have hoped for.'

CHAPTER 11

HOME PRIDE

The British Grand Prix is the home race for most of the Formula One teams, including Camel Benetton Ford, and, as such, bestows mixed blessings. Silverstone is as notorious for its queues of traffic as it is for its unreliable weather. Our friends from the Continent and beyond could be excused for thinking the British motor racing enthusiast has to be an insomniac with webbed feet, or simply a masochist. Whether you are working or watching, you have to be prepared for early mornings, late nights and any combination of elements in between.

This year, advanced ticket sales suggest the attendance will be down substantially on 1992. The effects of the recession are still being felt and there was a race at Donington earlier in the year, modest though the crowd was for that event. There has been a general sense of disenchantment with the entertainment value of the racing, and, perhaps most significantly of all as far as the British public is concerned, Nigel Mansell is no longer on the bill.

The drive to and from the circuit, then, is not going to be such an ordeal this time, but the team members haven't been spared the annual clamour for tickets. The Benetton boys have been grappling with the all-too-familiar problem. Kenny Handkammer says: 'People seem to think we can just come up with as many passes as we like. It's a pain. I honestly don't look forward to the British. I'm happy when it's over.'

Andrew Alsworth says: 'The tickets side of it is a problem, there's no doubt about it. We get two for Friday and Saturday or one for the Sunday. My girlfriend is coming up on Sunday. There's hospitality for them so it's good. They have a good day.'

Oz, as he is known to his friends ('It's sort of short for Alsworth and it was my dad's nickname'), does, however, take a distinct pride in playing his part for a British team at the British Grand Prix. 'This is our race, isn't it?' he reasons. 'And when you think about it, most of the teams are based in this country so really this is the home of motor racing. We have a long tradition in this and all speed sports. I was watching a programme about Donald Campbell and in an interview, just before he died, he was talking about Britain holding the speed records for land, sea and air, and it makes you realise what a history we have in these activities.

'The British motor racing public are great. They are real racing fans. They understand it and care about it. That's why they're prepared to be out there in the cold and wet, in all kinds of weather. The Ferrari guys can't quite work out the girls here, in their T-shirts and so on. But they, too, are real fans. I don't think there's a crowd quite like this one.'

Wayne Bennett shares Oz's pride. He says: 'The British Grand Prix does mean more to me than other races. It's nice to have your own crowd here and to see people you know. It's nice to be able to show them round the car and explain things, because a lot of the general public don't know what's involved at all. All they see is a car going round, they don't see the car close up and don't know what goes into putting the car together. It would mean a lot to me to have a win here.

'My wife is coming up for the race. You do get hassled for tickets by relatives and friends but you can usually swing a few deals. I managed to sort it out for my parents to come on race day as well, but obviously I owe a few favours now. I live down in Hampshire, near Winchester, so I stay in a hotel for Silverstone, in Bicester. It's not too bad a journey in. It takes about 20 minutes, a bit more on race day. We'll be up at about 5.30 on Sunday.

'I used to work on aircraft instrumentation, flight control computers etc. Then I worked at Tyrrell for four years and moved on to here in 1989. I am one of four electronics technicians on the race team. Two of us have Higher National Certificates in electronics and the other two guys have degrees in electronics. My job is to look after

Wayne Bennett taps into his world of electronics

any electrical component on the car and my specific responsibility is the active: programming the car, setting the active control, analysing data. Two of us do this, looking after the two drivers, while the other two work on the gearboxes.

'Obviously I would be sorry to see a lot of the technology go. I could be out of a job! I don't think we'll ever see the back of it, though, because there's still data logging to be done. You constantly need data on the car, to see how it performs, what it's doing at any time on the circuit. I don't think they'll ever do away with radios. You can't shout at a driver when he's in the car. Whether it will just be restricted to the pits, I don't know. I think it would be sad to see active and semi-automatic gearbox go. The driver is still the key figure. The car is set as a driver wants it and without that driver telling you how to set the car you're lost. I think it's an exaggeration to say a computer will eventually be running the car. There are so many different conditions and problems you could have out on the circuit that really a computer could never account for. The driver is still the crucial element. All you can do is make it easier for the driver to drive.

'Riccardo came here asking for semi-automatic gearbox so obviously he's keen to have that, and active. He'd become used to this technology at Williams and didn't want to drive without it. As for Michael, the more you give him the more he likes it and the quicker he goes. He has a mind to adapt to it. He's very good. He adapts to anything you throw at him and soon picks up how he wants it set and gets on with it. It's not just the basic ability to drive that is important, it's the ability to take on the technical stuff and make full use of it. The driver needs to know what the car is doing and what each setting does to the car, and both here seem to be able to do that and adjust the car as they want it.

'I don't think there's a serious danger I'll lose my job if all this technology goes. You just develop the car in other ways. To ban active, first of all they have to say what it is, then you just go to other things. You go to electronic roll bars and so on. You would still have some sort of ride-height, I believe, and you would still have some sort of semi-automatic gearbox. Traction control is never going to go because when it's developed you never know it's on the car anyway. There'll be no engine note change so you just won't know. There are always going to be jobs for electronics people in Formula One, and if not, there's always work connected with wind tunnel, testing... it just goes on. It's a highly sophisticated business and I think that's half its appeal.'

Schumacher the star on two wheels

Bennett is 28, married, with two children. 'It is a difficult life for a married man, the more so now we have young children. But my wife knew what kind of job I had and knew what she was taking on. Actually, it works out quite well because we get time off during the week, so I'm home with the kids then, when it's quiet. Weekends for me are too busy.

'After about seven years in motor racing it becomes just a job and you get into a routine. I was a fan before I came into this but I'd never been to a Formula One race. On race day I become a fan again. When they start, it still gives me a big buzz. I think our prospects here are very good. Okay, Williams are going to be very dominant, so all you can do is hope they have a problem and be there to pick up the pieces. I think it would make it more interesting if there were some showers. From my point of view, an unsettled weekend can double the workload. When it's wet and dry you're constantly going for wing changes from one minute to the next. Looking at the sky now, I'd say we could be in for a busy weekend.'

■ ■ ■

Michael Schumacher is busy on the Thursday, even before some of his main rivals have shown up at Silverstone. He takes part in a charity cycle race, organised by Camel, and wins the one-lap tour of the 3.247-mile circuit with, you realise, something in hand. The stragglers – who, in all fairness, would not claim to be athletes – are still panting their way through Vale as the lean German crosses the line. 'He should be over in France with the professionals,' mutters someone at the back, summoning just about enough breath to do so.

Vale, a dip and wiggle at the far end of the circuit between Stowe and Club, is one of the revised sections of Silverstone. The changes were carried out to make the old airfield track more interesting for drivers and spectators alike. There had also been calls to make it safer. Silverstone was the fastest circuit in Formula One, but two years ago the distinction passed to Monza. However, the new Silverstone retains hair-raisingly fast corners and offers a more severe all-round test for man and

machine. Leading drivers will tell you that it provides one of the sternest challenges in Grand Prix racing, physically and technically. And that very British added ingredient, the weather, serves to compound the problem. The wind, on this open plain, can play evil tricks.

Raw engine power is essential ammunition here, in the heartland of England, and Camel Benetton Ford are aware they will need all the muscle they can muster to take on Williams. They have decided, however, not to introduce Cosworth's latest evolution of the Ford V8, which includes new cylinder heads developed from the V12 programme, at this race meeting. The timing of its debut will depend on results of in-car testing.

The delay throws up the prospect of an intriguing tussle between Benetton and McLaren, the former permitting the latter to use the 'Series VII' engine here. The teams now have parity of horsepower and a voice from Benetton's ranks says: 'Now we'll see who can do what, won't we?' Confidence in the camp is rising by the race, just as Tom Walkinshaw predicted.

■ ■ ■

On Friday morning, 9 July, just five days after the French Grand Prix, practice for the British round of the World Championship begins. For some, at any rate. Tom, Flavio, Michael and Riccardo are huddled under the awning on the pit wall, anoraks zipped to the chin, hands thrust deep into pockets, shoulders hunched. This is the British weather the Continentals joke about, but there are few smiles. Rain is cascading from pitch-dark skies and bouncing off the circuit.

Benetton are in no hurry to commit their drivers and their cars to the perils of these conditions. If the rain eases then perhaps they will go out, but half an hour into the session there is no suggestion that the downpour is about to relent. A few cars do venture forth, giving the hardy souls out in the stands something to watch. Frankly, though, the exercise is futile. Damon Hill trails huge plumes of spray from his Williams and aquaplanes off the track at 180 mph, careering through the gravel trap at Stowe. Pierluigi Martini, back at the wheel of a Minardi Ford in place of Fabrizio Barbazza, smashes even more heavily into a barrier. Neither driver is hurt but Benetton have seen enough. They won't be venturing out into this. They abandon the pit wall, retreat to the garage and pull down the shutters.

Those who had to be out, the marshals and emergency crews, are soaked to the skin. The doctors, posted at strategic points around the circuit, have been equipped with rain gear which leaks. Formula One racing could not function without these people.

All the teams are functioning in the afternoon. Now, they have to: it's qualifying. It is still raining at 1 o'clock but, mercifully, there are signs it may begin to ease. Breaks appear in the clouds, though not before Mark Blundell loses control of his Ligier. The car hits a concrete wall and rebounds into the middle of the track. He is still in the stricken machine, contemplating his getaway, when he turns to see the two McLarens bearing down on him from the mist. Michael Andretti and Ayrton Senna react in formation, the American veering to the right, the Brazilian to the left. It is almost like a routine by the Red Arrows. Blundell knows he is a lucky man.

The session is stopped so that what is left of the Ligier can be dragged away and the track cleared. Conditions improve dramatically during the 18-minute hold-up and it is now obvious that further delay is bound to enhance lap times. By the closing minutes of the session slivers of blue sky appear over Northamptonshire and the traffic on the circuit is as heavy as any on the roads to Silverstone as the drivers cram in most of their permitted 12 laps. The rush of cars sweeps an almost dry line and the times tumble. At the end of the desperate scramble, the order is: Prost, Hill, Senna, Schumacher, with Patrese eighth.

Schumacher says: 'I did not see the point in going out this morning, but it meant we did not learn anything about the conditions. However, it did not take us long this afternoon. Maybe I went out a lap too early, as the track began to dry. I found the traction control was not exactly the way I wanted it to be and I could not really feel the car well. I think the Williams cars had an advantage with their ABS, too, which was perfect for these conditions, of course. Overall I would say we are maybe a couple of tenths of a second off where I think we should be on a day like this. If it is dry tomorrow, I'd expect us to be right on the pace again.'

Patrese is not too dismayed: 'In the conditions today, when everyone was waiting to go out at the end of the session, it was obvious that there would be a lot of traffic around. You would be lucky to find a clear lap. I don't think it was too bad. The balance of the car was okay. I could not choose the two or three laps I wanted because of the confusion with the traffic, but I think it was the same for everybody. It was all a bit of a lottery.'

■   ■   ■

Saturday begins with clear blue skies and no one minds the nip in the air. Urgency returns to morning practice, and although clouds move in and circle Silverstone by 9.30, there appears no immediate threat of rain and a dry track beckons. The teams have much to do, much to learn, and Schumacher is soon at work, eating up the tarmac. He leaves his marker: 1 minute 21.513 seconds. He and Patrese now pile on the mileage. Schumacher is third fastest, Patrese fourth.

There is a spring in the step of Schumacher and the Benetton engineers. 'The session has gone very well,' Michael enthuses. 'We have done the time we expected. Now it is dry we can hopefully improve our grid position. As for Williams, let's say we are not so far away from them as we were in Magny-Cours. We'll just have to do our best and see what happens in the race.'

With that he is off to the debrief. Everyone in the camp, Schumacher included, knows that, in normal circumstances, Williams are still out of reach, yet of the leading teams Benetton do appear to be on the steepest improvement curve. Certainly, they believe, they now have the measure of McLaren. The Woking-based team are 19 points ahead of them in the Constructors' Championship and Senna leads Schu-

Practice makes perfect...

macher by 21 points in the drivers' standings. Half a season remains; the gauntlet has been taken up.

Benetton's optimism is reinforced during qualifying, though not in quite the manner they had anticipated. Schumacher, pushing hard, clips the inside kerb going into Copse, the quick first corner. He wrestles with the steering wheel but cannot prevent the B193B hurtling across the track and into the barrier on the outside. He runs back to the pits and Patrese knows he must concentrate his own programme to leave his partner sufficient time to take over the team's only working car. A slight drizzle does not ease the pressure on Patrese but he posts a reasonable time and should be safely on the third row.

Schumacher, helmet and gloves already donned, sits studying the times on a monitor as Patrese's car is prepared for him. The Williams pair have claimed the front row but the third place on the grid is still on offer to anyone who can unseat Senna. Schumacher goes for it. He is, in full flight, a fabulous sight, and now he is in full flight. He soon moves ahead of Senna's 1:21.986, then chips away at his own time before settling on 1:20.401.

'I think we showed today how good the teamwork is,' says Michael. 'Thanks to Riccardo and the team I was able to go out and get third place on the grid. We had changed my car a bit for this corner but the wind changed in the afternoon and the car just got away from me. We had different wing settings and I found that Riccardo had the better solution, and that will make life easier for tomorrow. I didn't expect that to work so well. After I moved to Position Three I thought, now I can try what I want. I think the last lap was close to maximum. We also found out something useful about the set-up with full tanks this morning, so it looks like being a good race for us.'

Patrese is less certain about his car in race trim. 'Just like this afternoon, it was raining slightly so I could not get a good feeling for the car. But in the end we have fifth place on the grid and that is quite satisfying.'

■   ■   ■

The campers on Silverstone's infield and at sites around the circuit anxiously pop their heads outside for the first weather check of race day, 11 July. Again, the early morning is bright and clear, though we are warned there may be showers in the afternoon. That possibility will be considered when teams finalise their strategy for the race. All must be prepared to make swift, last-minute changes in response to nature's whim.

Rory Byrne, who seems to cover more pit and paddock ground than anyone, for once checks his stride to explain: 'The change of weather conditions this weekend has made it hard on the technical side because obviously you don't get as much time running in the dry or the wet. You find you've more work to do in less time. From our point of view it does make life more difficult but fortunately, with the active suspension, we have quite a wide range of adjustments, so we can dial the car in a lot easier than with the passive system. I'd say that in the wet we weren't as competitive as we have been in the dry, but to a large extent that was influenced by the decision not to run on Friday morning, when we thought the conditions were so bad it was too dangerous to run. There was too big a risk we would damage the car. Without a spare car now, that is one of the biggest considerations. If you go off and crash one of your cars and can't repair it before qualifying, you have two drivers sharing the other car and one of them is bound to be at a major disadvantage.'

Schumacher's performance in second qualifying indicates class will out, but point taken.

Byrne continues: 'We have some set-ups worked out should the race start wet and turn dry and vice versa, so we are reasonably well prepared. I think, basically, we are tending to prefer dry. I think we may be close enough to start putting pressure on Williams a bit because if you can't put pressure on them there's no way you are going to beat them. They are very reliable and while they can dictate the pace they are just going to be sitting there, one-two. But if you can start to apply pressure you might force them into an error, as Michael did with Prost in Monaco. He forced him to jump the start.'

Byrne, who also has responsibility for research and development, was assigned to Patrese's car to help the Italian through his early-season traumas. He says: 'It's all part and parcel of the job, coping with the drivers. You have to be concerned not only with the engineering but the need to relate to the driver. Above all, you must keep a cool head and analyse a situation rather than start allowing emotions to take over. It's almost a counselling job at times.

'There's no magic to the engineering exercise. The laws of physics still prevail and you've just got to work through that methodically. As far as the drivers are concerned, I believe in being quite open and straight with them. If we have a problem there's no point in sweeping it under the carpet. Admit it and work together to try to solve it. I suppose some drivers are difficult to contain but most of the good drivers aren't. They've been around long enough, they realise how complex the cars are and what difficulties can arise. They may not have the in-depth technical experience but I think they do have an appreciation of what it's all about.

'Michael is very cool and methodical, exceptionally so for a man of 24. He's an exceptional driver in every respect. His speed, his fitness and his stamina are remarkable. He won that cycle race at a canter, against people who cycle on a regular basis. I look at him and think, there's someone a bit special. It's very difficult to make comparisons, but Ayrton drove for us in his first year, 1984, and Michael has all the same attributes. Michael's going to be a world champion one day, I've got no doubt about it.'

South African-born Byrne moved to England in 1973 to help a friend compete in the Formula Ford series and the following year was offered the opportunity to develop a career as a racing car designer. At the end of 1977 he joined Toleman and, apart from a brief spell with Reynard's ill-fated Formula One project, has been with the team ever since. He says: 'Formula One is still as satisfying for me as it was when I first came in. When we started we couldn't cope. We had new engines, new tyres, new chassis – we just couldn't handle the combination of all these new things. It took us about two or three years to find our feet and start to make progress. The cars are so complex and the engineering issues that need to be researched so wide-ranging that you cannot possibly succeed as a small team. You've got to decide whether you want to be with a winning team or with a small team that runs well and is competitive occasionally but isn't going to get any further. But to be honest, the small teams that start to show promise tend to grow into big teams, which this one has.

'I find Formula One tremendously challenging technically. There's no limit to the technical challenge. There's so much you can do it's purely a question of the resources you have and the personal time and commitment you put into it. This will determine how much you can do and how successful you are. I wasn't racing last year and it wasn't really in the plans for me to race this year, but Riccardo was having quite a few problems early on so Ross asked me to come in and help out. It's not necessarily a permanent arrangement.

'I've got to do my job in research and development, and the conceptual work for the '94 car, so we're pretty busy. I don't know what, precisely, the '94 car will consist of because it's not been defined in engineering terms what we can and can't do. Until they do that I'm afraid everyone's going to be unsure. I won't necessarily feel frustrated if there are too many constraints on technology, because there are always avenues to investigate. You just work on different areas. It won't make any difference to the amount of money that's required or spent. The thing that is important is that the regulations are clearly defined in engineering terms to avoid confusion, otherwise we risk Formula One degenerating into a scenario like the America's Cup, where things are won away from the racing area, and that's in no one's interest.

'For me, what Formula One has to do is to improve the spectacle. We have to have better racing. I think the key to that is in actually looking at the racing regulations rather than the technical regulations. You could have pit stops for refuelling, even given the dangers. Modern technology and the size of the teams and the planning that can be done should ensure that the danger is contained. In the turbo days we had refuelling at high pressure, but so long as it is done by gravity and there are restrictions on hose sizes, everything is clearly defined and, above all, the pit lane personnel are controlled, then I think the risks, although still present, would be reasonably minimal. I would be happy to operate under those conditions and it certainly would improve the spectacle.

'Just another idea out of the blue – you could reverse the grid. You take the finishing order from the previous race and reverse it to determine the starting grid. It would make for some good racing. It's only a thought and I haven't considered the detailed implications. But there's no doubt we need to do something to improve the racing. At the moment it's just not interesting enough. Last week, Michael was the only driver in a leading position who overtook anyone and the television director missed it!'

■   ■   ■

The relative lack of congestion around Silverstone and the empty spaces in the stands confirm the suspicions that this British Grand Prix is not a box-office blockbuster. Of more immediate concern to the teams, however, is the weather. Three-quarters of an hour before the start, the clouds look docile and distant enough. The Camel Benetton Ford camp feel easier. A mechanic sits in the cockpit of Schumacher's car, revving the engine to the point where you think he must lift the roof off the garage. Ross Brawn ambles to the front of the McLaren pit, next door, and surreptitiously peeps through the throngs of photographers jostling for yet another snap of Senna, just to check what the opposition are up to. He turns back, apparently unperturbed.

Patrese appears, wearing an anorak over his race-suit. Schumacher turns up in race-suit only and is soon pulling on helmet and gloves. Wayne Bennett is crouching by Patrese's car, intently completing his programming with lap-top

Straight-line speed

computer. Schumacher guides the No. 5 B193B into the pit lane while Patrese waits for the signal from the pit wall that the systems are up and running. He gets the all-clear and ushers the No. 6 car out on to the circuit. They leave behind, in the centre of the garage, the spare car. It, too, carries No. 6, though a still sealed No. 5 sticker has been placed on the nose of the car, just in case. This week, however, the car will be idle.

Schumacher picks his way through the congested grid to his starting position, climbs out and sits on a covered spare wheel, chatting to engineers. Patrese moves into his slot, extricates himself from his cockpit and makes straight for Byrne, demonstrating with hand movements the behaviour of the car. If it is a crisis, Byrne won't be making a drama out of it. Engineers busy themselves, but then engineers are always busying themselves. A kind of Parkinson's Law tends to apply in motor racing teams.

The rain has held off but Prost has wheelspin at the start and loses his advantage, at the head of the field, to Hill and Senna. Schumacher is fourth, Patrese sixth. Andretti is off at the first corner. Senna is intent on making life as difficult as he can for Prost, slamming the door in the Frenchman's face every time he takes a look. Schumacher makes the occasional lunge at Prost, yet resists undue risk. The way the two in front are mixing it, he would be well advised to keep a safe distance. 'I wasn't too afraid something would happen,' he later says. Prost undoubtedly is and twitches alarmingly as Senna again retaliates.

Prost eventually gets by on the seventh lap, going into Stowe, and Schumacher accomplishes the same manoeuvre to go third, three laps later. 'I think Senna lost a bit of motivation when Alain took him.' The leading positions remain unchanged after the round of pit stops and Patrese finds himself competing with a batch of British drivers for the lower placings, when the contest is put on hold. The safety car has been sent out to form an orderly line while the abandoned Lola BMS Ferrari is removed from 'a dangerous position'. Many question that judgment and Schumacher confesses his surprise, yet adds diplomatically: 'We'd rather do something safe than something unsafe.'

The upshot is a 20-lap scrap. Hill repels Prost's initial attack only for his engine to blow. Schumacher, figuring Prost, too, might be vulnerable, turns up the heat. Similar thoughts are flashing through Prost's mind and he reins in the Williams. The gap between them comes down from 7.4 seconds to 4.1 seconds with nine laps left. Prost knows he must respond and does so. Michael can get no closer and accepts second place. Prost has his 50th Grand Prix win.

Patrese's aspirations change by the second. The safety car has left him to grapple with Brundle and Herbert for fourth place, while at the same time the three of them attempt to thread their way through back markers embroiled in their own skirmish. Brundle's resistance ends when his gearbox breaks, allowing Patrese and Herbert through to fourth and fifth places respectively. Riccardo has the beating of the Englishman and, to his amazement, inherits third place when Senna runs out of fuel in the final complex. It is his first podium place of the season and Benetton's best result of the campaign to date. Schumacher moves ahead of Hill to third in the Championship, Patrese up to fifth.

Prost and Schumacher, wreathed in smiles, congratulate each other as they climb from their cars. Patrese gratefully joins the celebrations. After the 'dry' ceremony in France, the British Grand Prix is awash in champagne.

Michael says: 'I'm happy for me and also for Riccardo. Second and third is really good for Benetton. The car was great today. We decided to go for high speed rather than downforce. I thought there was a little chance I might catch Alain and, although I always drive 100 per cent, I tried to push even harder. I thought maybe there was a problem in Alain's car also and drove to win, but he had everything under control.'

Riccardo concedes his good fortune, but reasons: 'Usually I have the bad luck so it was quite a pleasant surprise for me to see Senna had stopped. The first part of the race was quite boring for me so I have to say the safety car made it much more exciting. Suddenly I was in the middle of 20 cars. It was really quite wild at the end because I was fighting with Brundle and Herbert and we were trying to lap the back markers and they were fighting themselves. But for the first time this year I have really enjoyed the race a lot. I have not had a good first half of the season but everyone in the team has supported me. They have got a lot of passion. I hope this is the start of a good second half of the season for me.'

Schumacher and Patrese give Prost a party

Schumacher is now contemplating an even better result at his home race, in a fortnight. 'Maybe Alain and I will have a talk later and do a deal so that he will let me through at Hockenheim. There again, I think he would not be too happy with that.'

Undeterred, Patrese joins in: 'And maybe for Italy....'

The first three make for their respective camps and rounds of handshakes and back-slapping. There is great joy at Benetton, and particular pleasure for Riccardo. Rory can take immense satisfaction from the result. Flavio beams. 'Good, heh?' he says. 'And McLaren had the same engine....'

Up at the motorhome, team members' relatives and friends gather. They have had a good day, too. 'It means a lot to all the lads to have a result like this here,' says Wayne. 'It makes a hard weekend's work all worth while.'

CHAPTER 12

PEOPLE POWER

Talk in the build-up to any German Grand Prix is of power. The 4.235-mile circuit at Hockenheim is the most severe test of Formula One engines. Seventy per cent of the track is covered at full throttle. Raw, top-end grunt is essential, but then so, too, is reliability. Camel Benetton Ford plan to use the latest Cosworth V8 engines at some stage of the weekend, though they seem more likely to stay with the tried and trusted 'Series VII' units for the race.

Before all that, however, other issues are being considered in the corridors of Formula One power. An extraordinary meeting of FISA's World Council has before it reports from the Technical Delegate relating to the conformity of certain cars with Article 3.7 of the FIA Technical Regulations at the 1993 Canadian Grand Prix, and the conformity of the fuel used by certain cars at the Grands Prix of San Marino, Spain, Monaco and Canada. Benetton are involved in both instances. They accept the Technical Delegate's report on regulations but contest the report on fuel.

The World Council, confirming the earlier edict, rules that active suspension, traction control and anti-lock brakes are illegal, although teams will be permitted to run with the 'driver aids', under appeal, in Germany. Semi-automatic gearboxes are not to be outlawed. On the matter of fuel, the World Council concludes: 'The information and explanations offered by the competitors concerned and by the eminent experts from the relevant fuel suppliers have cast doubt on the accuracy of the tests which formed the basis of the Technical Delegate's report. The benefit of any doubt must always be given to the competitor. Accordingly, we confirm that the results of the Grands Prix of San Marino, Spain, Monaco and Canada stand.' Teams are warned, however, that in future they must provide fuel samples for approval before races.

All along, the feeling has been that FISA are intent on bringing teams into line for next season and that, at a FOCA meeting to be held on the day before first practice in Germany, Bernie Ecclestone will urge a compromise solution to avoid further blood-letting. The image of Formula One is taking another battering at a time the show can ill afford it, and Bernie knows it.

En route from Paris to Hockenheim, Benetton's attention switches to the Le Castellet circuit in the south of France, and there the subject of engine power surfaces again. Testing here is inevitably focused on speed and Riccardo Patrese's Camel Benetton Ford B193B reaches 334 kph (almost 209 mph) at the end of the awesome Mistral Straight. Word flashes around the Continent that Ford's 'Series VIII' unit does indeed have muscle to be feared.

All of which leaves Rory Byrne slightly amused. 'Yes,' he says, 'we did do that speed, but the papers got hold of the wrong end of the stick. It was the old engine. We were doing something else.' Whatever it was, it appears to have worked.

Yet again, it appears Bernie's power is working. The FOCA meeting, at a hotel near Hockenheim, is hard and long. We wonder if we should read anything into the thunderstorm raging above, but five hours after they sat down the team principals emerge with what is presented as an honourable settlement. It is now accepted that driver aids – except semi-automatic transmission – are illegal, but FISA will be asked to permit their continued use for the rest of this season. Bernie says that the teams realised the 'farce' had to stop, and that everyone had agreed to give up something to arrive at a compromise for the good of the sport. Details of the agreement for 1994 are not yet available because they, too, must be ratified by FISA. However, the inevitable leaks suggest that refuelling will be introduced and teams will be limited to 64 engines a season – or two engines per car at each race – in a further endeavour to spice up the action and reduce costs.

In the Benetton camp, Tom Walkinshaw welcomes the peace pact. 'It's good to get that out of the way,' he says, no doubt speaking for the majority of those directly or indirectly concerned with Grand Prix motor racing. 'Now we can get on with the racing for the rest of this season and plan for next season.'

The prospect of fuel stops causes some anxiety in the ranks. A technician confides: 'I have to say I'm not too happy about that. It would have to be very well organised. The guys would have to be all kitted out and the numbers in the pit lane kept right down to absolutely essential personnel. The risk of fire is obvious but it's not so much the fuel as the vapours. You can get a rush of fire along the ground and have your legs burnt. It's a shame about the active, too. But then there are always other avenues to pursue, and I expect we shall be going down them.'

■   ■   ■

All avenues in Germany, it seems, are leading to Hockenheim. Forecasts of more rain over the course of the weekend have done nothing to douse the enthusiasm or dilute expectations. Silverstone was like this last year, the fervour gathering momentum until it reached its giddy climax on race day; the circuit stands packed to the rafters, reverberating to the supplications of an unashamedly nationalistic crowd. Just as Nigel Mansell was exalted by British fans, so now Michael Schumacher is Germany's idol, and a congregation of 150,000 will be here to worship him in Sunday's Grand Prix.

The first wave of the faithful is already giving this Grand Prix the feeling of something special. Elsewhere, as we have seen, attendance figures have been less than spectacular, but the atmosphere and box office returns at Hockenheim are a reminder that the masses will always turn out for a home-grown superstar, and Schumacher is precisely that.

Here is a measure of the power, in sport and beyond, most precious and forceful of all: the power of people. Those supremely gifted and those who demand to see them must always shape the entertainment industry, and as so many in Formula One need from time to time to be informed, they are part of that industry. Its survival depends, ultimately, on its appeal to the public. Schumacher's appeal is now apparent as never before. In Germany he is up there with Becker, Graf and Langer. Perhaps he will be bigger than any of them.

In the Ligier garage, Martin Brundle, his former team-mate, considers Schumacher's form. The Englishman says: 'Right now he's driving better than anyone in Formula One. Senna looks as if he's backing off a bit, but Schumacher is doing the business. He's brilliant.' Ron Dennis, team principal at McLaren Ford, is equally impressed. He likens Schumacher to Jochen Rindt. Those who remember the sublime Austrian will know there could scarcely be greater tribute.

Schumacher disappoints none of his admirers in Friday's qualifying session. Despite the confidence of the Williams camp, Michael is up for the fight with ever more vigour. Several drivers come to grief at the chicanes which interrupt the long, narrow straights hacked into the forest. Positioning and the judgment of braking distances is crucial. Even Prost has his moment of uncertainty. The Frenchman and his British partner, Hill, as expected, lead the way but cannot shake off the pack as they had hoped. Schumacher strikes, splitting the Williams with a devastating lap.

The geography of this circuit – generally regarded as one of the least inspiring on the tour – is such that the young German has to travel most of its course again before receiving the appreciation of his supporters, awaiting his return to the stadium, which envelops the sequence of loops at the end of the lap. The delay makes his appearance beneath the great stands all the more dramatic. Fireworks and hundreds of German flags accompany him home. He salutes the spectators with clenched fist. And this is only Friday.

Hill is uneasy. He says: 'I don't want to be third on the grid. Not here. Schumacher is like a man possessed.'

Content, Michael certainly is. 'The car was perfect right from the start,' he enthuses. 'We haven't had to do too much to the set-up and any changes we made were positive. I might have been able to find a bit more time on my last lap but I had to back off when I came across one of the Lolas. But I have got to be happy with provisional second place. It's not often that you can say your car is absolutely right, but that's been the case today.'

His team-mate, Riccardo Patrese, has quietly gone about his work almost unnoticed. He is seventh on the overnight grid and simply says: 'No problems, really. I'm satisfied.'

This is also a race meeting of added significance for the Italian. Already by far the most experienced driver in the history of Formula One, he has now reached the landmark of his 250th Grand Prix. His team and sponsors will, of course, make an appropriate fuss of him and recognise the occasion with a convivial interlude, but the clash of celebrations is rather unfortunate. This is very much Schumacher's party. Not that Riccardo is unduly concerned. He is still savouring his third place at Silverstone. 'Perhaps,' he suggests, 'after the big fight I had there, people will stop asking me if I am ready to retire.'

Patrese made his Grand Prix debut at Monaco in 1977, driving a Shadow Ford. He had his first win at Monaco, five years later, with Brabham, and won again for that team in the final race of the 1983 Championship. He had to wait until 1990 for his third success, on an emotional day at Imola. By then he was driving for Williams and he had three more victories with them before switching to Benetton at the beginning of this year. A talented all-round sportsman, he is a formidable opponent on a football pitch, a tennis court and a ski slope. When he would rather do something less energetic, he enjoys messing with his collection of model trains or simply spending time with his family in Padua. He and his wife Susi have three children: a son Simone, aged 16, and eight-year-old twin daughters Maddalena and Beatrice.

■ ■ ■

The rivalry between Benetton and McLaren is heightened here by the availability to both teams of 'Series VIII' engines, and the new units are being put into the cars of Schumacher and Patrese for Saturday's practice and qualifying sessions. Deep into Friday evening, engineers, clutching pieces of paper, are scurrying back and forth between the Benetton garage and the Ford transporter.

Fellow Italians Pierluigi Martini, Andrea de Cesaris and Alessandro Zanardi (grouped left), Belgian Thierry Boutsen (blue shirt), Duncan Lee of Camel, and Tom Walkinshaw toast Riccardo Patrese on his 250th Grand Prix

Jim Brett, Cosworth's chief engineer with the team, is particularly active. And not a little anxious. 'In basic terms,' he says, 'I'm responsible for making sure the engines do their business at the right time for Benetton. Cosworth are contracted with Ford to build, supply and run the engines with Ford Electronics. We work together and generally have around ten people with the team at a race.

'We've had two engine changes tonight, both for mileage reasons and, in this case, to put the latest specification of engine into the cars. Therefore, we are going through checks and procedures at the moment to make sure that the set-up of the engines in the chassis is right, before we attempt to fire them up. There are obviously changes to be made because of the different systems involved.

'The normal work involves going through all the data of the day, checking all the electronics and making sure that all the systems have been working correctly and are going to work tomorrow. We want to make sure we get the most out of the engine. We check ratios, wings and fuel consumption variations for the different settings of the car: whether it is better to run less wing, less fuel, or more wing, more fuel. We and the team attempt to come up with the best combination and solution.

'Both drivers used the earlier specification engine today and it is intended that both will run with the latest engine through the day tomorrow. There is a chance they could run them on Sunday, but this engine is still relatively new. This is the worst circuit of the year as far as engine reliability is concerned, so it is risky to introduce a relatively new engine here. We haven't had that much circuit running with it yet. It has proved good on the dyno but there is no substitute for good circuit testing and we just haven't done enough of that. If the new engine proves a significant advantage tomorrow then we would have to consider the situation for Sunday very carefully. We would have to assess whether it was worth the risk of running it. The decision could be a difficult one.

'It is also difficult to quantify the potential of the new engine, but it has got more power at the top end. With this sort of engine development you have to sacrifice a certain amount at the bottom end, but at this circuit, where you are using high revs for so much of a lap, you need your power at the top. The new engine has an increase in power throughout that range, so it has to be better. But against that, as we have discussed, we must consider the reliability factor.

'The ordinary road user would never approach the limit of an engine's capabilities. The boy racer might, away from the traffic lights, where he gives it full throttle, but then he soon has to slow down or he's heading for a big accident. Grand Prix racing bears no resemblance to road driving. On any circuit a driver is on full throttle whenever he can be. Here, they are on full throttle, high revs, high speed, well over 300 kph, on, I think, four sections of the circuit. There really is no comparison between the two types of driving and the demands on the engine, or, indeed, the rest of the car. At this level of racing, if you are not on the absolute limit of everything, then you are not doing your job properly. Having said that, there's no point in getting more revs and power if you're going to get only halfway through the race. It is a very fine line between attaining the maximum from everything and finishing the race.

'These engines, and others, have a maximum usage of 400 km. After that the engine is worn out. It needs a total rebuild. An engine gets us through a Sunday morning warm-up and the race, and that is it. The engine then goes back to Cosworth, is stripped down, and everything is meticulously checked to find out what's happened to it and why. All the records and data from the race are gone through. Then about half of it is just dropped in a bin and thrown away. The engine is rebuilt with all the relevant parts. A rebuild, depending on the type of use – what circuit we've been to, how much abuse the driver has given it – will cost something between £20,000 and £40,000. It's very difficult to put a figure on a new engine because of all the development work and so on.' (General estimates put the figure at around £60,000 to £80,000.)

'These drivers use the engines, shall we say, to the maximum. All the top drivers will get the most out of the engine. There are some drivers, however, who are very skilled at taking care of their engines. Nelson Piquet, who of course drove for Benetton, is a good example of a driver who knew the value of reliability and getting the car and engine to the end of the race. He was much more gentle on everything. Michael is not bad; Riccardo is not bad. We have had worse, but they definitely do use theirs to the full. We have at this race 11 engines, partly because we have here the new engines.... '

At this point Brett is interrupted by a playful Flavio Briatore, apparently mimicking equine creatures seen outside the McLaren pit. This quest for horsepower is a touchy subject and Benetton are, after all, Ford's factory team. The man from Cosworth inevitably comes in for some ribbing. Jim, an affable, bearded, round-faced man, smiles and raises his voice as the mischievous Flavio strolls on: 'This engine is good enough for second place on the grid, but still some people are not satisfied.' *Touché*. Flavio laughs and disappears.

A more earnest expression returns to Brett's face as he continues: 'When an engine blows you have to accept it's all part of the business, but it is regarded as very serious. Cosworth is famous for its reliability and we like to think our engines are fairly bullet-proof. If something goes wrong the whole factory feels it. We want to find out why. The engine should not fail. We also supply a lot of customer teams who have to pay a lot of money for their engines and one way we can look after them is by giving them reliable, bullet-proof engines. It's very important. When a team is lucky enough to have a works deal, free engines, they can waste engines. But long term that can harm them, it can lose grid positions and points, so it is our duty to provide a reliable engine.

'We are very pleased with Benetton's performances this season. I think the team have done wonders this year, achieving what they have in such a short time with the amount of new technology that has gone into it. They have done a first-rate job. To be so close to Prost here, a driver of his calibre, is a truly outstanding effort.

'We must accept that Renault do still have that bit more grunt than we have. We never stop developing back at the factory. It is very difficult to keep getting more power, but that is what we endeavour to achieve. That process never stops. The proposal to limit each team to 64 engines next season will increase the pressure on us, although in normal circumstances we would expect to use only four engines per race, anyway. We have to get more mileage out of the engines while maintaining reliability and the same amount of power, at least, so it's not going to be easy. Oh, here comes the other trouble-maker....'

Jim Brett and the power behind Benetton's challenge

Now Tom Walkinshaw arrives beneath the Ford motorhome canopy and, like Flavio, cannot resist poking a little fun. 'Ah, but he takes it well, doesn't he?' says Tom, a devilish grin rippling across his face. 'He's a good guy.'

It patently helps to be thick-skinned in this business. 'The thicker the skin the better,' the beleaguered Jim confirms. 'We come in for a lot of abuse all the time. Whenever the car is slow, the engine hasn't got enough power; whenever the car is good it's because they've achieved a good set-up. It's the standard situation and has been so since time immemorial. And it will always be so.

'When lap times are good, we get just as great a sense of achievement as the team. That is what we are seeking, as well. What, after all, is the Championship for? It is not only for the driver to win. It's there for your engine to win, it's there for your car to win. If you're making one of the smallest electronic bits on the car, if you're machining the pistons, it's just as important to you to win. Everybody plays a part, even the sweeper-up. If he does his job properly then he keeps the boys happy because they are working in a clean environment, and so on it goes. All are part of the team, all play their parts, all want to be winners.'

Just then he receives a message from the pits: 'Ross Brawn is looking for you.' He raises a hand in acknowledgement.

'Excuse me, back to work.'

■　■　■

It is a little after 8.30 on Saturday morning and the earlier cloud cover is dispersing. Patrese is taking breakfast – coffee and bun – in the Ford motorhome compound. His son, Simone, is sitting alongside. Schumacher, already in his race-suit, strides purposefully from the Benetton motorhome to the pits. His urgency is evident all this second day of practice but so, too, deep into the afternoon's qualifying session, is his frustration. He has slipped to fourth, behind Prost, Hill and Senna, and cannot understand why he is not improving his time.

He retreats to the pits and waits, deep in thought. He has the laps in hand to launch another attack. But still he waits. A cloud cover is the signal to play that last hand. On used tyres, he hurls the B193B at the circuit, bullying it around the corners. He is on the very brink, but undeterred. The Williams pair may be out of reach, yet Senna's time of 1:39.616 is in his sights. He crosses the line on 1:39.580. More fist clenching, more fireworks and more, many more, flags. There are thousands of them. Patrese cannot improve on his time and is still seventh on the grid.

Michael says: 'This morning the new engine felt very good. They've done a good job. It is definitely better in top speed, as predicted, and this is especially important for this circuit. The next stage is to make sure it is race-worthy. I wasn't aware McLaren were using it since yesterday, which is interesting. I did a time in the 1 minute 39s this morning and felt sure it would be possible to go quicker this afternoon. I did what I thought was a good lap and it was 1:40. I thought, what was that? There was no explanation. I tried again and almost went off. I couldn't get the time. So I went in thinking maybe it will become cloudy or there will be some wind. Happily, when I tried again, I made it.

'Coming back into the Motodrome and seeing all the fans as excited as they were was an experience I have never known. Last year it was nice, but now it is so much more. They give so much to me. I'm sure they gave me the extra four-tenths of a second, because we did nothing to the car. The fans are making it such a special weekend for me. It is almost impossible to get in and out of the circuit. It is something I find hard to believe, something I could never have imagined.'

Riccardo, still quietly doing his own thing, sees a possible benefit in starting seventh. 'It means I'm just behind the potential confusion on the front three rows! So I think I'm well placed for a good finish.'

Jim Brett is also satisfied: 'Michael is very pleased with the top-end performance and I like to think that contributed towards his third place on the grid. At the moment we have no reported problems with the new engines. They are not going to be raced here by Benetton, and the previous specification, or even the one before that, would be more likely for Hungary. We are probably thinking more in terms of Spa and Monza for the latest specification.'

■   ■   ■

Schumacher is besieged whichever way he turns. He responds to microphones and autograph books with grace and good humour. This, now, is all part of the job. The job of a superstar. The man who guides his every move is the man who unearthed the uncut gem and is now Michael's manager. He is a former racing driver called Willi Weber.

For Weber too, ever gregarious, ever visible in team gear, this is a weekend out of the ordinary. He appears to be enjoying it. 'We have been six seasons together. I had a Formula Three team in Germany and always had to look for good young drivers to keep it at the top. In '88 I saw a young driver at Salzburg driving Formula

Centre of attraction... Germany's Michael Schumacher

Ford 1600 in an excellent way. It was completely impressive for me how this young man handled the car. I didn't know his name or what he looked like. All I saw was the number on the car. He left the grid in seventh position and before the first lap was finished he was in front by seven seconds. I said to myself, this man I need in my Formula Three team.

'I watched him in another two races, and then I spoke to him. I asked him if he was interested in testing a Formula Three car. He was completely shocked and said, why him? I said, because you need to show your talent in a Formula Three. We made a date for the test and after seven or eight laps Michael was one and a half seconds quicker than the driver I had in my team, with the same car, so this was the green light for me. This was the man I wanted and I immediately offered him a drive for two years. He said he didn't have any money for Formula Three, but I told him, 'I don't need your money, I need your driving; don't worry about the money, we'll find a way.' On the same day we made the contract, and this was the beginning.

'It was obvious he was an extremely good talent in the car because his handling on the limit was so impressive. It was unbelievable and my feeling was completely clear from that first day of Formula Three – that we would go together to Formula One. We didn't expect it so quickly, but we were well prepared. We made the choice of Mercedes and Group C rather than Formula 3000 and everybody thought, Willi is a bad manager. People think that if you drive Group C you are finished, you will never make it back to Formula One. But for Michael it was the right move.

'Then, at the Nurburgring, on the Saturday, I heard that Gachot was in jail and therefore Jordan would be looking for another driver for Spa. I thought, this is my chance and I will try very hard to get Michael in this one race, to show his talent. The Jordan car was a fantastic one at the time, and of course I knew what Michael could do. I knew Eddie Jordan from Formula Three and called him up and said, "I have the man for you." He said, "Who the hell is Schumacher?" I told him, but he said, "Oh Willi, come on." But I kept on at him and in the end he gave him his chance, and of course Michael was fantastic.

'We would have been happy just to put our visiting card on the pit wall for the future and leave, but then we had the situation of getting the Benetton car. This was the best chance we had and we did it immediately. The rest we know. It has been fantastic for Michael and I think it has also been good for the Benetton team.

'Michael Schumacher is a really big star now. He is on the way to putting Boris Becker a little bit on the side. In Germany we have not been used to having anybody like this in Formula One or motorsport for so long. I believe he will be Germany's first world champion. We have a plan – because as Germans we are always a little bit organised – that we will have a three-year learning period. It's not learning to drive, it's learning to handle himself and the situation and the politics around Formula One. In '95, it will be time to go for the Championship.

'It's 100 per cent my job to protect him, to keep his head clear for all the work he has to do at the race track, for talking to his engineers, for time for the car, for the race, and keeping well prepared. I was a race driver for 20 years so I know the problems. The moment you are distracted too much, you are a second slower. So it is one of my biggest jobs to take all the pressure away from him and just leave him in peace. I do everything I can to let him live a happy life, because if you are happy you are strong and this makes you better for racing or whatever you do. His earning potential is up there with Becker and Graf, but you have to be very careful here in Germany with sponsorship and commercial involvement because if you do too much it can become overkill. From our first two or three days together we agreed it was the motorsport we wanted to build up. When we are good, the money comes by itself.

'His popularity now in Germany is very strong, of course, and there are heavy demands from the media. Sometimes when there are 20 or 30 journalists waiting for him back at the motorhome, I ask him if he would prefer it if there were only one, and he agrees that I am right, really. Sometimes I have to remind him of this. I think we do quite a good job together. We came into Formula One like a team, in a way it had never happened before, and the first thing I did at Spa was to organise a press conference, for one hour. This we still do and it takes a lot of pressure from him. The journalists don't have to hunt for him and follow him to the toilet to ask him something. He is here for everybody, and this arrangement makes it easier for him, too. It is not always easy for me to organise things but I love to do it. And it's a very nice job.

'I don't really have to be hard with Michael. He's a young man but he knows what he wants. He's very strong, and he needs to be, otherwise he will never be in front. But he's hard-working, like me, and we both know what we want. We want to be on top and we are willing to do the hard work that is necessary to take us there. We are both surprised things have happened so quickly. The first time he was on the podium I was crying. It was so fantastic for me. Now I get used to it and I'm waiting for it. It's a normal situation that he's on the podium. If he wins here … oh yes, I'll be crying again.

'Michael is a man who can change immediately. Sometimes I think he is two persons. After he leaves the race track he is completely relaxed, and this is one of his strongest points. Other drivers, like me for instance, took a week to get over the race, whatever the result was. With Michael, the next day he is completely out of it, and this makes him strong. His fitness and enthusiasm come back like a battery charging up very quickly.'

Michael is charged up for this one, yet not to a state of frenzy. He copes with the rounds of briefings – and the constant requests for a picture, an autograph, a handshake – with consummate composure. Out in the campsites, heads are not so clear. Strong beer and warm evening sunshine prove an intoxicating mixture. But then, this is all part of their big race, and the toast is: Michael Schumacher.

■ ■ ■

The first daylight hours of Sunday 25 July are seemingly locked into the night. Sombre skies and flashes of lightning beckon the traffic along the wet autobahns towards the small, neat settlement of Hockenheim, and into the circuit. Any racing track takes on a more sinister, even gruesome aspect in the rain, but none more so than this one. Spray hangs eerily in the forests, like curtains fiendishly obscuring cars ahead. Such conditions were to end the Formula One career of Didier Pironi here as he turned his Ferrari towards the forests one Saturday morning in 1982. He ran into the back of Alain Prost's Renault and was launched over the top of it, sustaining terrible injuries. His appetite for speed still not satisfied, he was to die in a power-boat accident. Jim Clark, one of the most revered drivers of any generation, was killed in a Formula Two crash here in 1968. And yet there is something in

The pace and precision of Patrese's pit stop

Hockenheim which tantalises the racing driver, separating him from the rest of us. Damon Hill says: 'There is a certain crazy thrill about travelling at more than 200 mph down a narrow road with trees either side. You do feel you are riding a bullet.'

Hill is particularly concerned about the bullet to be ridden by Schumacher. Less than a second covers the first four cars on the grid and the Englishman fears Michael could break the Williams monopoly. Benetton confirm that both their drivers will run the 'Series VII' engine, while McLaren have a 'Series VIII' for

Senna and a 'VII' for Andretti. Senna, comprehensively beaten by Schumacher in recent races, clearly feels he has nothing to lose and possibly something to gain.

Dick Scammell, head of Cosworth's racing operation, endeavours to clarify the situation regarding the supply of their latest engines. He says: 'Our agreement is with Ford and within that agreement we are able to supply the latest specification engines to both Benetton and McLaren. Both teams have three of the latest engines here. From there, it is up to them. We do not intend to get involved in team strategy.

'What people must never forget is that this is a highly competitive situation and feelings can run high. The competition this weekend is good. We're closer to Renault. The 'VIII' is giving more top-end performance, as it was designed to do, but I think you'll find teams being more selective with their engines. Just as an athlete prepares and specialises for a particular event, so engines will be refined and used for particular circuits. Our work on the V12 has gone quite well and we're waiting for the new regulations to be published before we can determine its future, but I have to say that the way cars are going now, things seem to be less in favour of the 12.'

Dick Scammell

Cosworth's racing division, based at Northampton, employs 450 people and is responsible for building and developing power plants for IndyCars and lower formulae and categories, as well as Formula One. The dominance of Ford Cosworth in Formula One was broken in 1983 by the new wave of engines, the turbos. Scammell says: 'By the time we started with a turbo it was too late; Grand Prix racing was about to revert to normally aspirated engines. But now we have a good new challenge and we are rising to it. Our racing business is good and that, after all, is what it is. Our engines are leased to teams – apart from the factory team – on a package basis, and next year we'll be offering a two-tier service, depending on the financial means of the team. In the end it comes down to cost and what the team can afford.'

Warm-up is about to begin, and although the storm has receded the morning is still wet, the track and forests still treacherous. A few minutes into the session, television captures Derek Warwick's Footwork, shorn of its two right wheels, bouncing along the guardrail like a demented bronco. It crosses the track at a chicane and flips over. Mercifully the Englishman, with help from marshals and Jean Alesi, is able to scramble clear, and after a hospital check he decides to race. He had run into Luca Badoer's Lola, the slower car confronting him, from the mists, in an instant. The horror of Pironi almost replayed.

We are spared further major incident or anxiety, and by lunchtime patches of blue sky brighten the scene. Flavio Briatore peers from beneath a peaked cap and asks: 'What is this weather going to do? Maybe it is going to be okay.' As far as he is concerned, everything is now okay on the engine front. Standing at the entrance to the Benetton motorhome, his greying locks cascading from his cap and framing his brown face, he says: 'I don't care what McLaren have or what they do. It is better for the sport like this. Look at yesterday – four cars close together. This is how Formula One should be. All this business about engines, fuel, etc., etc.... We don't need it. We don't need the politics, we need stability and we need racing. When Schumacher beats Senna they say it's the engine or the fuel. Now they cannot say that any more and still Schumacher will beat Senna, you'll see. Look at this crowd; this is for Schumacher, just like Silverstone last year for Mansell. This is for a racing driver and a car, not for politics.'

■   ■   ■

Mexican waves and tens of thousands of German flags produce a carnival atmosphere in the Stadium as the drivers climb into their cars and await the opening of the circuit, at 1.30. Schumacher and his Camel Benetton Ford are lost behind a mass of photographers. At last he emerges and heads down the pit lane. He returns, however, with news of a problem and is pushed back into the garage. The car is lost again, this time beneath engineers. Others scurry about the spare car, and a set of tyres is hurriedly wheeled in. Clearly, it may be pressed into service. A technician says: 'Looks like something electrical.' Then another says: 'A problem with the active.' In five minutes the pit lane will close, so a decision has to be made. The frowns indicate they cannot be sure of sorting out the problem. The spare it must be, and Michael switches from one cockpit to the other. Even a police officer is jostling for a snap, but now all are cleared from the front of the garage and Schumacher drives down the pit lane again. This time he continues to the grid, noisily picking his way through to his place. His crew are ready for him and consume every remaining second to make further checks.

It is a potential setback, though perhaps more psychological than actual. Drivers tell you they feel more comfortable with their race car. They just do. It doesn't matter now. Michael is in the spare, and at the first corner he is second. Prost has had another bad start and Hill leads. Senna attempts to bully Prost, only to spin at a chicane and drop to the back. Patrese is sixth, behind the two Ligiers. Prost, his resolve fortified by that skirmish with the Brazilian, closes on Schumacher and takes second place on the sixth lap. On the eighth he is in the lead. However, the Frenchman, along with Brundle and Aguri Suzuki, is given a stop-and-go penalty for missing a chicane on the opening lap. When they settle down again, the order is: Hill, Schumacher, Blundell, Patrese, and then Prost.

Schumacher makes his strategy clear when he comes in for fresh tyres at the end of the 16th lap. He will push hard and make a second stop at roughly two-thirds distance. He slips to fourth, but soon takes Blundell for third and posts the fastest lap to date. Towards the end he is accepting third place, just as Patrese is resigned to sixth. But, on the penultimate lap, Hill's passage to a maiden Grand Prix victory is again sabotaged, this time by a puncture. Victory goes to Prost, second place to Schumacher and fifth to Patrese.

Michael celebrates as only Michael can, and his countrymen in the huge, curved stands join in the festivities. 'The crowd has just been fantastic and crazy all weekend and at the end of it all we have a great result, although, I must admit, a little lucky. I was a little worried about switching to the T-car because it was not quite as good as my race car, but that was jumping around down the straight and as we could not find the reason we decided to change.

'I was surprised all weekend how close I was to Alain, and it was the same in the race. The two tyre stops made it possible to push hard and I thought maybe at the end I might be able to put some pressure on Alain. If I had known Alain was staying on the same set for the whole race I might have stayed out on my second set, but during the last laps I was hearing a funny noise from the engine so it was important then to finish the race, and when Damon stopped it was a nice surprise for me. Last year I was third here, this year second, so maybe next year I will be first.'

Riccardo, too, has had his complications but, like much of his weekend, his race has been a relatively private affair. 'My car was fine with the first set of tyres but with the second set I started to have problems under braking,' he reveals. 'The rear wheels were locking and the car was jumping around and feeling strange on the straights. The steering wheel became stiff and the car was oversteering. I don't know where the problem was coming from; maybe something was wrong with the tyre pressures. I went straight on at the first chicane because my rear wheels locked and I was lucky to be able to keep the car under control. Altogether, I am happy to bring two points to the team.'

Those two points help Camel Benetton Ford close to within six points of McLaren in the Constructors' Championship and give Patrese fifth place outright in the drivers' standings. The top of the two tables now looks like this: Constructors' Championship – Williams 105 points, McLaren 53, Benetton 47, Ligier 19, Ferrari 10, Lotus 10; Drivers' Championship – Prost 77 points, Senna 50, Schumacher 36, Hill 28, Patrese 11, Blundell 10.

Home is the hero

CHAPTER 13

KEEP ON TRUCKIN'

The three-week break between the Grands Prix of Germany and Hungary gives the teams an opportunity to take breath or even a rest from the treadmill of the World Championship. Work goes on, of course, but with a little flexibility, it is possible for Camel Benetton Ford's drivers to seek recreation. Michael Schumacher finds his fun on the doorstep at Monaco, while Riccardo Patrese pops over to the island of Sardinia. Ross Brawn, too, manages a sojourn, in France. FISA have confirmed the changes to the regulations for 1994 but not yet in sufficient detail to convince Benetton's technical director that he and his men can commit themselves to a design and direction for next year.

Rory Byrne says: 'We can't really plan for the next year because although we know what is illegal we don't know what is legal. Until they define it precisely we can't really act. Sure, we're doing work in the wind tunnel, but at this stage we can't really go any further. It would be nice to think we're going to get some stability in Formula One at last, but we haven't had any for ten years so why should we now? The thing is that all of us are so used to the constant changes and the uncertainty. We can't afford to be thinking totally about next year, anyway, because there is so much more we want to achieve this year. We want to keep improving, win a race or two and finish second in the Championship. That adds up to a lot for us still to do with the car this season.'

Schumacher, mixing business with pleasure, underlines the team's undiminished commitment to this year's campaign with another productive test at Silverstone. He tops the time sheets, using the 'Series VIII' Ford Cosworth engine, while Allan McNish concentrates on set-up for Hungary. The cars for Budapest will have the 'Series VII' engines and feature slight yet important modifications to the active suspension and traction control systems, as well as significant aerodynamic changes, intended to provide maximum downforce. 'Yes, it's gone pretty well,' says Byrne. 'We've moved forward, but then so have the others, make no mistake. Usual story, really.'

It doesn't pay to get carried away in this business. Still, it does seem Benetton are on a roll and no one is more encouraged than Schumacher. He can have a few days' relaxation before heading for Budapest, his confidence soaring. He is a man in form and Hungary might, just might, be his race. He doesn't advertise the prospect, but that is how he feels. So, also, do other members of the team. Benetton will be setting out to the Hungaroring with high expectations.

■   ■   ■

The Hungarian Grand Prix begins eight days before the green light for Benetton's other drivers, Dave Hughes, Martin Pople, Jon Harriss and Kristan De Groot. These are the men responsible for delivering the team's two trucks, carrying the cars and equipment, to the circuit. They leave the factory on the morning of Saturday 7 August, take the cross-Channel ferry at Dover, and drive down through northern France to Reims for their first overnight stop. The journey across Europe takes them into Germany on the Sunday and a second halt at Nurnberg. On day three they are into Austria and that evening they cross the Hungarian border. The final leg of the 1,300-mile trek, on Tuesday, brings them to a race track carved out of rolling countryside, near the Hungarian capital. The yellow and white, 16-metre Scania trucks are backed up to the pits, along with the Ford Cosworth rig and those of all the other teams. It is an impressive line-up and will remain in place until after the race.

Hughes and Pople drive the truck carrying the cars, Harriss and De Groot have the support truck. Driving is just part of their work. They are responsible for load-ing, unloading, and setting up the garage. Then each has his job over the race week-end. In essence and spirit, however, they are truckies; a breed apart.

Harriss, 28, is in his fourth year with Benetton. He says: 'Hungary and Portugal are the longest trips we have. We had a good drive down, no problem. Life on the road is something I wanted and all I've done since I left school. All I wanted was to drive for a racing team. I am a racing fan but there's no racer in me. There's too much to throw about with these things. The

Benetton's other drivers... Left to right: Jon Harriss, Kristan De Groot, Dave Hughes and Martin Pople

appeal of the job is not having a boss. We get on well with each other and with the other truckies. We normally travel with Cosworth and a couple of other teams.

'Our truck carries most of the equipment, mechanics' tools, spares and a machinery centre – lathe, drill, grinder etc. When we get to the circuit we wash down the trucks and set up the garage before the mechanics arrive. It's up to the four of us to make sure everything is there, ready to go. We put up the banners, get out the cars and equipment, get the tyres and fuel and make sure it's all in place. With the races outside Europe we still have to do all the packing up, and take the stuff to the airport for the flight, then set up things at the other end. I'm also responsible for Michael's tyres. I get them fitted, marked by the scrutineers, and see to the tyre pressures and temperatures. If we make a mistake then obviously we get it in the ear, but I like to think we don't make too many of those.

'On the road we used to get held up a bit at the customs, but not now the bor-ders are open. There can still be a little delay into Hungary. Last year the trucks were searched fairly thoroughly three or four times at Dover, coming into the country. Obviously there's been a lot of concern about drugs.

'I'm married, with family on the way, but then they do say absence makes the heart grow fonder. I was testing before I came racing and that makes life much more difficult, not knowing when you are going to be away. Doing this, I can work out my season and plan my life much better. I think the mechanics would say you have to be slack to be a truckie. They rib us for being out on the road and getting more expenses, but then we point out that they have an extra four or five days at home. On a trip like this, for instance, we are away 11 days. They are away for a standard race schedule, five days.

'One drive I don't look forward to is the one down to Monaco because there's so much hassle there. It's a good drive to Estoril because it's not all motorway. These things are very easy to drive. They are like motorised armchairs. They've got cruise control, air conditioning, CD, everything is riding on air, so it's not bouncing up and down.'

Hughes, a 43-year-old from Anglesey, North Wales, first joined the team in 1980. He is known on the road and up and down the pit lane as 'Yoss', a nickname he has had since Yosser Hughes achieved national fame in the television series, 'Boys from the Black Stuff'. Although he drives with Pople, he rooms with Harriss, who is 'Cheesy' to his mates. (That name stuck after he used the word to describe how he felt at the end of one particularly long, hot day at work.)

Yoss left the team to join Leyton House a couple of years ago and moved on from that sinking ship to another, a Formula 3000 team. 'Luckily, I was asked to come back here,' he says. 'I jumped at the chance. There are lots wanting this kind of job. I'm sure there's a massive pile of applications back in the factory. Everyone you meet on the road asks how I got into it. I did general haulage before I came here. I didn't take a car licence until I was 24 and just got to enjoy driving. Now I'm nearly 44 and I can't imagine another life.

'We are a bit of a clique, really. We arrive at a place earlier than everyone else, we meet on the road and eat or have a beer with the others. We stick together quite a bit. I was married, but not any more. I think, basically, this game was to blame. It gets like a trap. You start earning good money, with expenses and everything, and it's quite a good life, and once you start, it's very difficult to stop. I've had a girlfriend for the last couple of years and things are okay. She understands the job situation.

'Within the team we get on really well. At Leyton House, it wasn't too bad, but it didn't have the atmosphere of Benetton. Some people like driving fast cars, I like driving trucks. You wouldn't catch me going anywhere near a racing car. I suppose there has to be something different about racing drivers. Look at Michael. He's got to be completely crazy, hasn't he? He's very good. I fancy him to do well here. I am Riccardo's tyre man and I find him a very nice guy. I don't have as close a relationship with him as his mechanics do, but he does know I'm his tyre man.

'I certainly wouldn't swap places with a mechanic. We gave the other guys a bad time because they had a really hard day getting here. They left at five in the morning and didn't get here until five in the evening because of a problem with the

The Camel Benetton Ford racing team

flight. We get back to the factory from this trip on Wednesday lunchtime but I find the actual driving relaxing. These trucks are wonderful. They are so powerful you hardly have to change down. One or two guys in the past have acquired reputations for being a bit reckless, but they didn't last long. With the value of everything we're carrying, you're aware of the responsibility. Most of the guys are very professional. If I wipe out this truck it's not only the truck itself, which is worth more than £300,000, it's the three cars and spare chassis. The three cars are built up, with engines, ready to go.

'The worst incident I had was back in '84, when we had only one truck and I had no co-driver. I was going down through Spain, to Estoril, and thought my brakes weren't working too well. I was going down a nasty hill, into a gorge and, not having driven the road before, had no idea what was at the bottom. So I decided to save my brakes until I got to the bottom, in case I really had to anchor up. It was lucky I did because at the bottom was a sharp right turn on to a narrow bridge across a river, and I only just made it. That was scary.

'I worry sometimes about security, leaving the truck overnight, but nothing has happened to me so far and these trucks are quite secure, anyway. We have alarms fitted and the back door has a double bolt. They are obviously very distinctive trucks, with all the names on and everything, and when we are standing on the dockside, waiting to get on the ferry, no end of people come up and ask all sorts of questions. If it's a truck driver it's "How did you get this job?" Others, going on holiday, want to know where we're going. That's those who don't know anything about motorsport. Those who do will say something like "You did really well in the last race" or "Have you got any stickers?" or "Have you got any T-shirts?" and so on.

'I don't know how much longer I can do this job. I really don't know what I would do next. I don't think I could do it until retirement age. It's getting a bit hard now. Fridays are okay, Saturdays are not bad either, but Sundays are hard. By the time the

Dave Hughes... happy to let Patrese do the driving here

race is over, we've finished loading the trucks and driven a couple of hours up the road, it's a long day. I've always maintained that when we win the World Championship I can retire then. Whether that will happen, I don't know. It's nice to see the team progress. I've seen them creeping up and I was there in Mexico when we won our first race. Now we're knocking on the door this season. I'll give it a few more years, anyway. It would be a nice way to go out, though, with the Championship.'

De Groot, 24 and single, doubles up as the man in charge of the equipment. His name is Dutch, his nickname, Ripley, is taken from the *Alien* movie character. He explains: 'I shaved off all my hair last year and that was it.' Alien fans will doubtless understand.

So how do Ripley and Cheesy split the driving? Ripley replies, with a grin. 'If he's got a hangover, I drive; if I've got a hangover, he drives. No, I like driving in the morning. For the other guy, that's kip time or the chance to do whatever he wants to do. We try not to set hectic schedules because we can't afford to be whacked when we get to the circuit. On this trip we've planned the hotels in advance. Normally we don't bother, we pull over and see what's available. But you can be looking for somewhere until the early hours of the morning, so I prefer to have somewhere to head for. You can plan each day and make sure it's not too heavy.

'When you've travelled all day in the cab with someone it's nice to have someone different to talk to in the evening. That's why we switch things and I room with Martin. It can get trying at times with the same guy. [Laughs all round as Cheesy listens in.] This is my third year with Benetton. Before that I had two years with Nissan sportscars. It's good, really good.'

By now all four truckies are gathered at the front of their rigs. A couple of them are sitting on the tyres, laid out on the tarmac, one is leaning on a tyre trolley, another on a cab. They are joined by a truckie-cum-tyre man from Williams, who recalls a slip-up in his team for which he was responsible. Management and drivers appeared understanding and told him not to worry, to get on with his work. After the practice session, however, he received the mother and father of a dressing down. 'I'll keep out of the way in future,' he concludes.

Yoss is reminded of a time-consuming error leaving the 1986 Hungarian Grand Prix. He says: 'It was the first time we came here and we were going straight on to Austria for a race the following week. We pulled out on Sunday night thinking we'd get as far as we could. We stopped at a hotel and got up the next morning thinking, "Great, we're ahead of everyone else." We had seen no one on the road at all and set off again. Then I saw my mate looking at the map, and turning it round. Suddenly he said, "Stop, stop. The lake is on the right, it should be on the left!" In the night we'd taken a wrong turn and we were heading towards Yugoslavia. That cost us about four hours.'

Cheesy: 'What about Kris. He managed to get into the wrong truck one day. Course, they are so similar and they're parked together. He gets in and sits there, wondering where his briefcase and tapes are.'

Pople is '29, almost 30, and definitely not married'. At the circuit he becomes the fuel man. 'I like Formula One and I like travel, so I suppose I couldn't have a better job,' he says. 'As truckies we do get to see something of the countries, whereas mechanics just see airports and race tracks. I'd like to be a racing driver. I do some rallycross when I get time but this is a bit above my league. You've got to have money to get into it and then be in the right place at the right time. I think I'm getting a bit too old now, anyway.

'On the road we do four-hour stints, which is not too much. Legally, you're allowed to do eight-hour stints with a break, but that's too much. The hours we do in a day depend on where we're going, the route and whether we have a special need to push on a bit. Normally, we do about 11 or 12 hours a day. We had a hard time at last year's French Grand Prix, when the lorry drivers' blockade was on.

Because we normally travel in small numbers it was easy to stop a truck and hold it. The Jordan engine truck got stuck and they threatened to torch a fuel truck. The truck drivers, farmers and police were apparently all part of the same union, so the police were directing us into the blockades. Instead of taking us four or five hours from Calais, it took us about 24. I went ahead in a mini-bus to find a way around the blockades. Coming back all the team trucks travelled together in convoy, through the night, lights flashing, to Le Havre. It was quite a sight.

'At the circuit I deal with setting up the garage, all the banners, air lines for the fuel pumps, setting up the pit wall assembly. I pick up fuel barrels from the Elf truck, and I have to work with the engineers and Cosworth. It's a three-way thing. Whatever they ask for, I have to have it ready and pump it into the cars. I think it's the only job now where one person is dealing with all three cars. Sometimes it gets a bit hectic. When two cars come in together and want fuel at the same time, I'm running around like a headless chicken.

'If something goes wrong the management put it across to the person responsible to buck up his ideas and make sure it doesn't happen again. I was quite surprised how calm the drivers are. They sit there in the car when things are going wrong, but then they know we work hard and things are going to go wrong occasionally. It's certainly not often. It's important for a team to have a set sequence for everything and that everyone knows his job.

'There's so much that goes into a team, behind the scenes, that the general public don't appreciate. People tune into the BBC on Sunday afternoon, watch a two-hour race and think that's all that happens. It can be a boring race and they switch off not too impressed. If they saw a bit more of what goes into the weekend, particularly qualifying, I think they'd get a different impression. Some people would get more enjoyment out of qualifying than the race. The drivers are pushing themselves harder, the cars are quicker. The team in the garage is working harder, too. That's where the whole team aspect comes into it. There's a real buzz, it's great.

'It's nice for us to be up there with the front-runners. We're getting results and getting closer to Williams. We're probably the best of the rest and looking good for this race.

'It's a life that suits me. The truckies and motorhomers move around together and stop together. Then, at the end of the European season, at Estoril, we have a truckies' and motorhomers' party, the night before the mechanics get there. That's always one to look forward to.'

■　■　■

Benetton are looking forward to this race. They sense Williams will be within their reach on this climbing, tumbling, meandering circuit. Martin Brundle described the Hungaroring as a street circuit in the country. Schumacher was strong but unfortunate at Monaco, that most famous of street circuits; perhaps his luck will change here. Patrese has been consistently competitive here, qualifying and racing well. Fortune, however, has not been his travelling companion, either. Maybe this time.

Practice on a hot Friday sustains Benetton's hopes. Schumacher leads for much of the morning session, launching his B193B with utter conviction. He is eventually nudged off the top spot by Alain Prost's Williams but is still hugely satisfied. Patrese, less spectacular yet no slouch today, is third, ahead of Damon Hill's Williams and Ayrton Senna's McLaren.

Patrese puts one in the bank early in qualifying, while Schumacher – like Prost – bides his time. Michael is still sitting in his car, monitoring proceedings as the Frenchman steers out onto the track. He goes fastest, then faster. Several cars come to grief on this notoriously slippery circuit, where clouds of dust settle and set their traps. Senna is among the victims and complains about the positioning of the kerbs. Officials will later agree to lay concrete extensions at three of the corners.

Schumacher is unrestrained. He cannot match Prost's time but beats Hill to second place. Patrese is fourth, Senna fifth. Michael is ebullient: 'From the minute practice began this morning, we were on the pace. We were able to build on that and develop the car for qualifying. At past races I have complained about problems with the traction control, but after that test at Silverstone I can say that 99 per cent of the trouble has been solved. It was working fantastically well today, which is a big help on this circuit. It was a brilliant effort from everyone.'

Friendly rivals... Alain Prost and Michael Schumacher

Riccardo isn't quite up there among the superlatives, yet appears to be at peace with the world. 'Fourth fastest time; no problems, really. The car is good and the only trouble I had this afternoon was when I came through just after Warwick's spin. That meant I couldn't use my second set of tyres properly.'

Prost has provisional pole and the chances are he will still be there at the end of the second qualifying session. He has not, however, been as reliable at the starts, and on this track – as at Monaco – all are particularly keen to lead at the first corner. Prost anticipates assaults from his team-mate, Hill, from Senna and from Schumacher.

What, you may wonder, are Prost's impressions of Schumacher? Does 'The Professor' view the charging youngster as an upstart? Does he feel Michael dances too close to the edge? The responses are intriguing.

Prost says: 'He's at the level I and the team expected, but he is much quieter, happy and enjoying what he's doing. On the podium you see it. Even when he's second or third, he's always happy, and this is something I like to see in a driver. At Silverstone you could see it and he came to congratulate me after the race. But it is there also when people don't see it, at testing, for instance. Very often we talk together and not about the racing. We talk about bikes or something like that. I like this kind of relationship. It hasn't happened very often in Formula One in recent seasons. In fact, drivers talk to each other more than people think, but not so much the top drivers once they are starting to fight for first place. When they are competing together like this it is a bit more difficult. But that is not the case with Michael, and I am quite pleased he is like this. It is good for us drivers to be like this. It is good for the image of Formula One. It is important for the sport that the public sees good ambience between the drivers on the podium. It is much better than it has been in the past.'

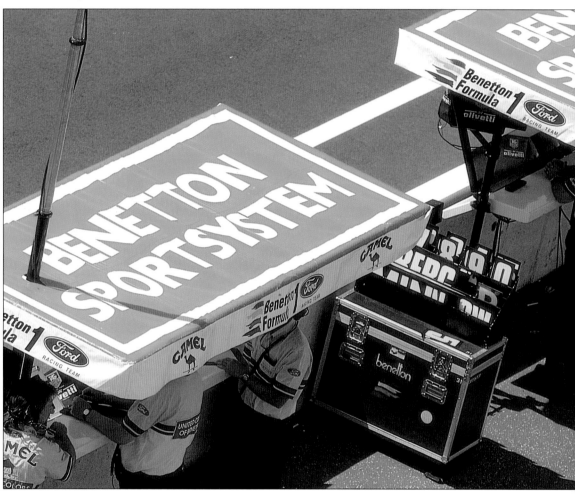

All set up for work

Senna has not been mentioned in the context of the conversation so far but do we not hear the contrast coursing through Prost's words?

He goes on: 'I don't consider Schumacher as a young driver, without experience. I consider him as a top driver. When I am in the car I don't think he has had only two years in Formula One or anything like this. I regard him more as I do Senna.

'I don't worry for him that he is on the limit. At Magny-Cours last year, for example, he showed he can make some mistakes, but someone else [Senna] was involved. This year he had a few problems at the start and I suppose it was understandable. He had no traction control. I don't like to compare drivers, to say he is better than this one or that one. It is difficult, anyway, because of the different cars and so it may not be fair. Certainly you can say he is one of the best to come through in recent years and I think he could be a world champion. He has the ability and I think the character, the attitude. These things are just as important. Even more than the driver I consider the man. I like him, I think Formula One is good for him and he is good for Formula One.'

■　■　■

Benetton's team members open their hotel room curtains on Saturday morning and take in the view across the Danube. The rising sun gives the sky a pinky hue and lights up the beautiful old buildings of Buda, perched on the hill at the other side of the river. This is one of the great and captivating capitals. Schumacher, alas, is not so enthralled. He has not slept well and insists on changing his room for a second time. The noise of the air conditioning disturbs him but cool rooms are not easy to come by at the height of a Continental summer. Top sports people tend to be susceptible to colds and bugs. You wonder if they are hypochondriacs. Experts tell you they are finely tuned athletes who simply cannot function at their best if their systems are slightly out of synch. Maybe the truth lies somewhere between the two theories.

The upshot is that Michael is no longer on a high and it shows. He is not himself. At the end of the day he is not second on the grid, either. He has slipped to third, behind Hill, while Riccardo is down to fifth, behind Senna. Michael says: 'I am a little disappointed, but I expected Damon to be quicker and that's why I went back to third. This morning we ran the car with very little fuel for a while and it was very promising. We were on old tyres so I felt very confident that the car would be good, but for some reason it was difficult to do the time I expected and I'm not sure why. There was a vibration from the car and I don't know what that was, either. Still, third place gives me the better side of the grid, the car is good in race trim and my starts seem to work quite well – we'll see. It should be interesting.'

Riccardo puts his problems down to traffic. 'The second run was the worst – slow cars, yellow flags, people spinning. But even on my first set, I was not able to get a completely clear lap and that meant I couldn't concentrate 100 per cent on a perfect lap. It is a pity because I feel sure I could have at least matched Senna's time.'

Over the course of the weekend, Patrese has been involved in talks with Flavio Briatore about his future. For weeks there has been speculation that he would be released at the end of the season and it is one of many suggestions doing the rounds here. There is more talk of Benetton switching to Renault engines, of Mansell replacing Patrese, of Senna replacing Patrese. What does now seem clear is that someone will replace Patrese. The Italian effectively concedes as much, saying: 'I am concentrating on the final part of the season and then we shall see if I go on with Benetton or maybe with another team.'

It just hasn't worked out as the driver or the team had hoped and the tough decision has had to be delivered to him. Flavio confirms: 'There is a mutual agreement between Benetton and Riccardo to free everyone for next season. It has been done in a very friendly way. I am free to sign someone else, he is free to sign for someone else. We will finish the season in the right way.'

■　■　■

Sunday 15 August is expected to be the hottest day on record in Budapest. A sobering thought for the drivers as they begin the countdown to the race. Schumacher looks more sprightly again, Patrese much as ever, and the team still have the feeling this could be their day. Schumacher bolsters that optimism with the second fastest time in warm-up. Prost is still fastest, Hill third, Senna fourth, Alesi fifth, Patrese sixth.

As race time approaches, the temperature is up to 37°C. It is going to be a long, gruelling afternoon for the drivers and their teams. Pople takes a breather, wafting his blue trousers. Benetton personnel – unlike their main rivals, Williams and McLaren, and other teams – are not allowed to wear shorts on race day. The team prefer a truly uniform turn-out. Pople says: 'It's going to be a lot hotter for the drivers, though. I think Michael's fitness could tell out there today.'

Gordon Message is of like mind: 'As far as fitness is concerned, Michael is in a class of his own. What he needs, though, is a good start. The last thing we want is for Senna to get ahead of him.'

Senna is renowned for being difficult to overtake, especially on a circuit such as this, and he could be a formidable barrier between Schumacher and the Williams pair. All of which heightens the tension in the Benetton camp. It is a discernible tension. It is also evidence of their expectations today. Those expectations are raised still further when Prost stalls at the start of the parade lap and is relegated to the back of the grid. Schumacher will have a clear run to the first corner, on the side of the track which offers more grip. Even before the start, things are going his way.

The start, though, does not go his way. Hill again races clear and Schumacher, in his eagerness to make amends at the first corner, attempts an over-ambitious line with cold brakes. He drifts wide and, by the time he scrambles back, he is down to fifth place. Ahead of him: Hill, Senna, Berger and Patrese. Schumacher takes his partner on the second lap and closes on Berger. Down the straight at the beginning of the fourth lap, the Benetton lines up an attack on the inside, only for the Ferrari to cover. Schumacher reacts instantly, switching to the outside, a bold manoeuvre. Yoss Hughes' words come to mind: 'He's got to be completely crazy, hasn't he?' But then, as Hughes also said: 'He's very good.' Michael proves it, making the pass and moving up to third place.

The adrenalin pumping, he now over-reaches. He is desperate to get to Senna. Too desperate. The No. 5 Benetton leaves the track and, although Schumacher manages to bring it back, he is now down to tenth place. He resumes his charge and, on the 17th lap, passes Alesi for fifth place. On the 18th he gains two places. He overtakes Patrese and benefits from Senna's retirement. Another lap, another place, repeating the earlier manoeuvre, to remove Berger from his path.

Schumacher is 40 seconds down on Hill, but he's flying. At the end of the 23rd lap the gap is 23 seconds. Schumacher's pit stop promotes Patrese to second, and that is where the Italian will stay. The German exits the track again on the 27th lap and this time he does not come back. He departs not merely disappointed, he is crestfallen. Dejection envelops the camp. It might have been. It really might have been. But not now. The shrugs and expressions say it all.

Patrese's cup of joy

Michael is in no mood to hang around. As he gathers his things, he says: 'The car was really good, balanced exactly as I wanted it. I made a mistake at the first corner and lost some ground. Then I spun when the rear wheels locked as I went down to second gear. I spun again when I had to move quickly to one side as Andretti suddenly slowed in front of me. There was dust and small stones everywhere in the car and the engine stopped.'

Jim Brett, of Cosworth, adds: 'Michael suffered an auxiliary systems failure.'

Patrese, meanwhile, maintains a consistent pace to secure that second place, his best finish of the season, ironically on the weekend he has been released by Benetton. Hill, his luck finally changed, has his first Grand Prix win. Riccardo says: 'I remembered that Damon has been having bad luck and thought maybe this would give me a lucky win. It was not to be. In any case, second place is very good. I let Michael overtake me early on because that was the strategy. My plan was to play a waiting game because this is a long, hard race. My only problem was when I lost third gear about 25 laps from the end. That is the most important gear here, but I had a big advantage over the cars behind me, so I was quite safe.'

Schumacher has slipped to fourth, behind Hill, in the Drivers" Championship, but Benetton are now equal second with McLaren in the Constructors' standings. Five races left and all to play for.

For those other Benetton drivers, the Hungarian job is still far from over. They have to load up the trucks and then take to the road again for the long journey home. They will have earned a weekend off.

CHAPTER 14

HOLD YOUR BREATH

No current race track in Formula One sets the pulse racing like the Spa-Francorchamps circuit does. It is the longest, most beautiful, spectacular and awesome course on the World Championship tour. Every driver will tell you its high-speed climbs and swoops through the forests of the Ardennes represent the challenge that always stirs them. Many are invigorated by Monaco, Imola or Silverstone, but Spa is THE favourite. The scenery and dimensions bring romance and theatre to the home of the Belgian Grand Prix. Fans pour in from across Europe, pitching their tents among the trees on the hillside. They come in droves from Britain and this year in their thousands from neighbouring Germany. Schumacher mania is taking hold again.

It all started here, of course, two years ago, for Michael Schumacher: Formula One debut, instant acclaim and a switch from Jordan to Camel Benetton Ford. Twelve months ago, he reached another landmark here: his maiden Grand Prix victory. 'The emotions I have for this circuit are something special,' he says. 'The feelings are of excitement... it is fantastic. I feel now almost as if I have three home Grands Prix – Monaco, where I live, Germany and Spa, which is closer to my home town of Kerpen than Hockenheim is. I can't believe what has happened to me in the last two years. It has been like a dream.'

Schumacher, however, is a realist and has no fantasies about his prospects for this weekend. 'Everybody is expecting me to say I have a good chance here, but the situation with this circuit is like Hockenheim. Practice went well there, but in the race we had no real chance to fight against Williams. I think it will be similar here. A podium finish would be a good result for us, but I don't expect to win unless something unusual happens. We should, though, have more top end power because I expect to be racing the latest Ford engine here. We have tested it and it has gone well enough.'

Riccardo Patrese, fresh from his second place in Hungary, is seeking more points. 'The car goes well on this type of circuit and Benetton tell me they are traditionally very good at Spa, so I hope the tradition goes on. The active suspension is important here and you have to know how to get the best performance from it. Now we have a clear picture of the car and how to make it work on any type of circuit, so we come here with lots of confidence.'

The plan is to use 'Series VII' engines on the Friday, 'Series VIII' on the Saturday and, if all goes well, race with the latest spec for the first time. Schumacher is also keen to use a new, automatic starting mechanism, which the team have been secretly developing. The idea is to give the driver the advantage of maximum throttle from the grid. All he has to do is keep his eyes on the lights and push the 'up' paddle of the transmission system when they change to green. In 17 practice starts at Silverstone it worked every time. Patrese is reluctant to take it on board but Schumacher is receptive to any innovation.

This latest piece of wizardry serves to illustrate the constant search for technological improvements. The changes to regulations for next year challenge the designers to find another means of achieving the same results. All the teams are particularly anxious to find a way of compensating for the loss of active suspension. Ross Brawn and Rory Byrne have made the point: 'How do you define active suspension?' The task now is to reproduce its advantages with a legal car. Drawings are already stacking up back at the factory. A further complication for Benetton is the lingering uncertainty about the engine situation. A different engine would necessitate a different design.

■   ■   ■

Friday 27 August. Early morning mist and a chill in the air. You settle for that at Spa. Rain is an habitual hazard here, rendering an already daunting circuit perilous. The forecast, though, is promising. We could be in for a dry weekend. The mist lifts and the temperature begins to rise for first practice. Time for a first look at Eau Rouge. This is perhaps the most fearsome section of race track in Formula One. To call it a corner won't do. The cars plunge down the hill from La Source hairpin, flick left, then right at the bottom and sweep up the steep gradient at the other side. Martin Brundle says he has never watched here. 'It's best not to,' he reasons.

Alessandro Zanardi, the former Benetton test driver, is exiting Eau Rouge at 170 mph when he loses control of his Lotus Ford. He hits the barrier on the left, the explosion on impact

Spa... beautiful and awesome

ripping away all four wheels and demolishing much of the bodywork. What is left of the car spins like a top across the track into the barrier at the other side. He is knocked unconscious and has to be carried into an ambulance. He is taken by helicopter to hospital, where he will be detained overnight. He will miss the race but, although sore and badly shaken, is otherwise unhurt. He knows how lucky he has been. Once again, the safety cell of a Formula One car has done its job. It takes more than an hour for the buckled barrier to be replaced.

Frank Dernie observes: 'The best thing ever to emerge from rule changes is the crash test. All the rest has been bull by comparison. We've taken drivers' feet further from the front of the car and ensured cars absorb impact. A head-on, into a solid object, at 40 mph and you're dead. With a road car you want something which will absorb an accident rather than one which is solid and doesn't give.'

Before the end of the morning's session we have another alarming moment. Philippe Alliot's Larrousse runs wide out of Eau Rouge and up the kerb on the left. He manages to bring it back but the car careers off at the other side. He is able to climb out of his cockpit unscathed.

Allan McNish, a current Benetton test driver, is watching here. 'Every word you can think of describes Eau Rouge. You just hold your breath. It's the most

Schumacher... a blur at Spa

amazing sensation.' The general feeling among drivers is that the authorities should provide an adequate run-off area on the outside but that the corner itself should remain unaltered. This unique challenge must be protected.

Schumacher and Patrese come through the first day without great drama, the German provisionally qualifying third, the Italian sixth. Neither, however, is content. Problems with the active suspension have hampered the Benetton and Michael is one and a half seconds down on the Williams pair, Hill and Prost.

Michael says: 'The car felt unstable and was not handling well, in particular at Eau Rouge. During the last two years I have taken Eau Rouge flat but not today. So far I am 95 per cent. The cars are 20 kph quicker. We are doing about 290 into the corner.'

So how does he describe the experience of Eau Rouge? 'When you arrive there in sixth gear, you know you have the chance to do it flat. You just see the first turn, you don't see the exit out of the corner. You go in, your foot still on the throttle, and if you can keep it there you feel so good when you know you have done it. It is a fantastic feeling. You block out the fear. It is more sensational than frightening. You have not too much time even to think about it, anyway. I would say it is the greatest corner in Formula One.'

In an attempt to sort out the active problem, the team decide on a software revision and work deep into the evening. The improvement through Saturday comforts Schumacher and he produces a dazzling display in qualifying to close on Williams. Prost and Hill respond and, at the end of his second run, Schumacher is disappointed he has not made more ground. He is still third, while Patrese has slipped to eighth.

Michael says: 'When I saw the time I have to say I thought it was surprisingly slow, missing about half a second. So I don't know what happened. I saw the yellow flags in the final section where someone spun off, in the Bus Stop chicane, and there is a chance I slowed down a bit there. I went sideways as I accelerated.'

Time out for Schumacher

Riccardo says: 'This was not a smooth session for me. I have had problems all day with the throttle and, when I was trying for a quick time, towards the end of the session, there were yellow flags and traffic. I wanted to be further up the grid because I wanted to run an attacking race, but from here, maybe I will have to be a bit conservative.'

One piece of the team's strategy is in place. Jim Brett reports no problems with the latest specification engine and confirms that both cars will race with it.

■   ■   ■

Into the evening, the bars and restaurants of the locality are enjoying brisk trade. You'll find some of Europe's outstanding eating establishments in this region. And the Belgians have made their chips – as well as their chocolates – probably the best in the world. The forest campers are preparing supper when their attention is caught by the slim figure appearing in their midst. Schumacher, leaving the circuit for his hotel, decides to take a detour to look in on some of the German fans. They

*Patrese and Schumacher parade
in style*

Right: *Schumacher emerges from
the plunge at Eau Rouge*

can scarcely believe their eyes. He spends more than half an hour with them. He has a drink, chats, signs autographs and poses for pictures. It is the happy, smiling people's hero we are now accustomed to seeing on the podium; it is the open, communicative driver Prost contends is good for Formula One.

Michael says: 'I think my attitude is to be easy, be true, be honest and laugh when you have reason to. This comes back to the team. It's a very relaxed situation. Everyone works and talks and laughs together. It is a relationship you don't see in many teams and we are fortunate to have it here. I think

Michael unleashes a series of fastest laps and closes the gap to 2.6 seconds. He even dares to take Eau Rouge flat. 'If anybody could, I knew it would be Michael,' says a mechanic. The team are on their toes, their eyes flashing from monitors to

Schumacher and Hill celebrate their great race

track and back again. Hill responds with a new fastest lap. The 38th time round Hill goes faster and Schumacher faster still. It is a stupendous duel, worthy of the setting.

Alas for Michael, and the team, he can get no closer to the Williams. Second place it is. Riccardo is sixth and their combined scores enable Benetton to move four points ahead of McLaren in the fight for runner-up position in the Constructors' Championship. Williams, as expected, have sealed the title.

Schumacher says: 'The car was fantastic and terrific to drive. I am sure that if we had not had that problem at the start, I could have pushed hard and got myself into a winning position. It was, as Alain is teasing me, a "Prost start". It is very difficult to do the job if you are coming from behind so I plan to make a big improvement, if possible, for the Italian Grand Prix. I think we can be close again, if not closer, to the Williams there. But congratulations to Damon. We had a brilliant race and he did a fantastic job.'

Patrese says: 'We both did our maximum, but unfortunately we both had trouble at the start. I am happy we are second in the Championship and now I am looking forward to Monza.'

Up in the pits, no one is finding it easy to mask the disappointment. Heads are bowed, shoulders hunched. Schumacher has produced one of the most pulsating drives of the season and yet.... The frustration of Hungary has been compounded. This time they were so close, so tantalisingly close. That start will be the subject of an investigation back at base and, at Monza, they will hope to have it right.

No one is more dejected than Flavio Briatore, but he senses the need to give the troops a lift. 'It is the first time we are really able to challenge Williams, you know. Michael was fantastic.'

And yet. This is a hard game.

CHAPTER 15

SIGNS OF THE TIMES

There was a time, not so long ago, when you approached the Italian Grand Prix, at Monza, with searing excitement and no little trepidation. If you had any soul at all, this was the most awe-inspiring cathedral in motor racing. Many will swear you had only to walk into the old place to see, and hear, the ghosts of great races past.

The legends live on in the hearts and minds of the faithful, but most come here to worship Ferrari and of late that faith has waned. The Prancing Horse has not been on the podium for almost three years and the *tifosi* harbour scant expectation of success this weekend, even if Jean Alesi, on the back of encouraging test work, is declaring his confidence. The crowd is likely to be modest in numbers, the atmosphere unexceptional. Even on the Thursday, there ought to be a tingling sense of anticipation. There is not.

Flavio Briatore, ever an opportunist, never a shrinking violet, suggests Benetton is the bandwagon of the future and indicates that Italy's racing enthusiasts are already jumping on board. 'We are the alternative to Ferrari,' he says. 'We now have 300 fan clubs and this is growing all the time. We are consistently beating McLaren and Senna, with the same engine, and at Spa we beat Prost. We have done this with hard work and a good team.'

Schumacher... for once in the shade

Briatore's optimism is fuelled by confirmation that he and Richard Grundy have finalised a two-year sponsorship deal with Japan Tobacco. Grundy is beavering on other fronts to secure the team's financial base and reinforce their ambitions.

By the end of the first day's practice, however, some of the wind has been taken from Benetton's sails. Both drivers have been unable to find an effective balance and here, on Formula One's fastest circuit, in damp conditions, confidence through the corners is crucial. Michael Schumacher is sixth on the provisional grid, Riccardo Patrese a distant 18th. What's more, Ferrari are flying. Alesi is Williams' closest challenger and milks the applause of the gallery. There are, of course, knowing nods of heads in the pit lane. Well, this is Monza....

Schumacher is more concerned with his own car. He says: 'I am struggling, particularly through the first Lesmo. Every time I go into the corner, I don't know where I am with the car. It feels like it is going into the barrier. The car is jumping around and there is not much grip.'

■　■　■

The annual Camel Denim Press v Photographers football match that evening offers some urgently needed relief for the two Benetton drivers, though not before they exchange anxieties over earlier proceedings. 'There is a real problem with my car,' says Schumacher, shaking his head.

'It is the same for me,' says Patrese, lacing up his boots. 'I just can't get it to work.'

They take out their frustration on the opposition, helping the scribes to victory after a penalty shoot-out. Not content with converting his team's first penalty, Michael then goes in goal to make the vital save.

The game is just one of the many off-track commitments the drivers have over the course of the race meeting. Almost every minute before, between and after practice sessions is accounted for. Each has a work schedule typed out for him when he arrives at the circuit, detailing meetings, sponsors' engagements and media interviews. This may be Patrese's home race, with all the emotional significance that embraces, but Formula One's most experienced campaigner accepts it is still another weekend at the office.

Different sport, same celebration

Patrese says: 'In the last part of my career there has been more and more work away from the circuit. It is the way of modern Formula One. From Thursday morning to Sunday night we don't have much time of our own. I don't think it is too much or that it affects my driving. People in other jobs have to work long hours and I have work I enjoy. Sometimes it is hard when you have to go to see sponsors and their guests after a bad day, but you try to be polite and professional. Formula One is very expensive and the money comes from the sponsors.

'There is now more effort in public relations and even to drive the car is harder than it was at the start of my career. Physically, it is more demanding. You must be more of an athlete than the drivers of 20 years ago. I eat in a way that is good for me, but it is not so much the diet as the training that is important. You can eat something extra as long as you burn it off.

'The other big change during my career has been the improvements in safety standards. It is a subject we always discuss and everyone is doing a very good job on this. An accident such as the one Alessandro Zanardi survived in Belgium would, I think, definitely have been fatal when I started. But the new, young drivers must never think they cannot be hurt. You can never feel 100 per cent safe in a racing car. Even at 100 kph an accident can be serious if the angle of impact, and the luck, are against you. I don't worry, otherwise I would stop. But now, more than ever, I know that a Formula One car can be dangerous.'

Relationships between team-mates in Formula One are often strained, even hostile, but Patrese has an excellent rapport with Schumacher, just as, in the past, he had with Nelson Piquet and Nigel Mansell.

Patrese... speaking his mind

Riccardo says: 'My philosophy is that it is better to build a nice relationship because it is in my interest, in my team-mate's interest and, above all, in the team's interest if we have a good atmosphere and no problem between us. I have always believed this and always had good team-mates. I don't play politics and maybe that is one of my problems, because in Formula One sometimes you win with politics. I have been around for many years, of course, and I have not won as many Grands Prix as Senna, Prost or Mansell, but at some points of my career I think I could match them and beat them. But I don't think I was as good at politics as they were, especially Prost and Senna, and even Nigel in the later years.

'I think Nigel suffered in the first part of his career, when he was not able to play politics so well. Because these drivers like to play politics, they have problems staying together in the same team. I am not saying I am the nice guy, but I play my cards on the table, not under the table. Maybe I will not be remembered as a world champion, but I would like to be remembered as a person who always said what he thought and never played funny games with anybody.

'I think Michael is going to be the champion of the future. I knew he was very good. I could see that last year. Any driver who comes into Formula One and after his first full season has a win and finishes third in the Championship has to be good. And remember he did not have the best car last year. He was ahead of Senna and Berger and they both had better cars. He is improving all the time. This year he has the confidence, he knows he is very strong and he has 120 per cent motivation. He is in his explosive moment. From the speed point of view, he is already maybe the quickest with Senna.

'It is not so much his speed as his maturity which has surprised me. He always talks a lot of sense. I have never heard him say a stupid thing, the sort of thing you would expect from a 24-year-old. Perhaps, though, he will have to improve on the politics. It seems that if you want to be world champion you must play politics and be a little on the bad side, otherwise you find this world is very tough. But I don't see any young ones at the moment who can match his pace.'

Riccardo found it tough trying to establish himself as Schumacher's partner. He concedes: 'I was not really happy at the halfway stage of the season and the team were not happy because I was not having the results. I could understand their point of view. It was difficult for me because I did not have much winter testing and we had a new project, but there was no point going on for another year like this. So we reached a settlement freeing us to do what we want next year. If they find something better for them, they can take it; if I find something better for me, I can take it. The situation is open.

'Since then, in fact, things have improved. In four races I have got 13 points, which I don't think is bad. It is clear I don't have Michael's speed, but I play more of a waiting game. He is fourth in the Championship, I am fifth and Benetton are second in the Constructors' Championship, so overall we have a good balance.

'I have the enthusiasm to go on for another year, especially now that we are going backwards a little with the cars and taking away the electronics. It will be more like the configuration of 1991, when I had my best season. I think the Williams last year suited Nigel more and the Benetton this year suits Michael more. I am happier when you have to feel the car more and have to tune every-thing. So I think that next year I can be in a competitive mood and I want to prove it. When everybody has to drive more, maybe I can come up again.'

■ ■ ■

More overnight rain leaves the teams to contend with a wet track on Saturday morning and contemplate inadequate race preparations. Ferrari, who of course have been able to test here, are able to maintain their advantage over all but Williams, and Alesi secures third place on the grid, his day marred only by a bizarre collision with his team-mate, Gerhard Berger. The Austrian, though dazed, is uninjured and will line up sixth, behind ...d Schumacher. Patrese is tenth.

...'s improvement is consoling yet far from satisfactory for a team now ... in on Williams and outstrip the rest. Schumacher reports: 'We ... of the problems from yesterday but, unfortunately, not enough. ... the bumps from not having the right balance and enough ... swer to that right at the moment. The first Lesmo was ... going in the right direction but, because of all these ... rning, we are not able to think too much about the race set-up. At least we are usually good on full tanks so we'll have to wait and see what the race brings and how we are in relation to Ferrari when it really matters. It should be interesting!'

It is much the same story from Patrese's side of the garage. He says: 'The car was very difficult to drive. It still does not have the right balance. We have to work very hard on this because there is still improvement to come. Of course, I am more satisfied today because I have a better grid position and, from there, I still have a good chance in the race.'

■ ■ ■

Another storm accompanies darkness in the area stretching up to the lakes and mountains, but by day-break on Sunday 12 September the skies are clear and we can confidently look ahead to a dry race. The half-hour warm-up session takes on added importance and at last Schumacher is into his stride. Patrese remains unhappy with his car and decides he will race the spare.

Both cars have the latest Ford Cosworth engines but Schumacher decides against using the automatic starter which caused him so much grief in Belgium. He looks composed, his crew easier. Tom Walkinshaw says: 'What with the wet and dry conditions in practice we've not been able to get on top of it. But we seemed to do that this morning and Michael was very fast.'

Renewed confidence is evident in the stands, too. A banner displayed by a group of supporters reads: 'Benetton – the start of a legend.'

As technicians complete their chores on Patrese's car he prowls, pensively, at the front of the pit. Even now, the PR work goes on. He dutifully poses for pictures with guests, forcing a smile. At last he can get on with the driving. He takes the car on a couple of laps before coasting to his place on the grid. He stands in the shade of an umbrella, talking to Frank Dernie, and then to Briatore. Finally, he has a brief word with his wife, Susi. They part with a kiss. Their son, Simone, still lingers at the front of the car as Riccardo pulls on helmet and gloves.

The waiting over, the cars are sucked into the first corner, a chicane inevitably trips up someone. Hill and Senna have a coming together, t' are able to continue down the order. Prost, Alesi and Schuma mêlée. Patrese also comes through unscathed, seventh in the o

Schumacher passes Alesi on the fourth lap and appear to the podium when, on the 22nd lap, his engine ble B193B. The rueful German says: 'Compared with t' perfect this afternoon. I really believe we had heard a horrible noise from the back of the ca

CHAPTER 16

VICTORY AT LAST

The Portuguese Grand Prix, the climax of the European tour, has long loomed as a potential landmark in Camel Benetton Ford's season and guarded optimism accompanies team personnel, smartly attired in dark blazers, on their British Airways flight to Lisbon. Recent disappointments are too vivid in their minds to allow expectations to run out of control, but all logic suggests this could be the one. The configuration of the Estoril circuit, with its sweeping, plunging bends, should suit the B193B and bring the Williams into its sights. All they require now, it seems, is a little luck. All!

Considerable changes have been made to the circuit, just a short drive inland from the coastal resorts of Estoril and Cascais. A new pits complex has been built

Binned up and ready to go

and about half the track has been resurfaced in an endeavour to eradicate the worst of the notorious bumps here. Not all the facilities are quite in place yet, but then this is Portugal and the pace of the country is part of its charm.

This corner of the universe has its compensations, not least its fish restaurants. Ross Brawn manages to get out late on Thursday evening, relishing a quiet meal with his wife. He should have known better. It is full of Formula One folk, including drivers Karl Wendlinger and Derek Warwick. Ross is loudly teased by the entire restaurant when he gestures away the obligatory flower seller. The mischievously gallant Warwick steps into the breach and, with great ceremony, presents the slightly embarrassed Mrs Brawn with a rose.

Morning comes too soon and with a bit of a shock. They've messed with the clocks here and fallen into line with the rest of the Continent, which means we're all making for the circuit in darkness. Most of the Benetton boys have had breakfast by the time the sun begins to creep over the hills and sprinkle daylight on the track. Martin Pople is a little behind the rest, sitting alone, scooping up his baked beans. He has been busy improvising over at the pit wall assembly. He explains: 'They've raised the barriers at the pit wall so high we couldn't see over them. We needed something to stand on. So, down to the local supermarket, a few plastic bins, just the job.'

It seems to have escaped the planners' attention that the teams like to keep an eye on proceedings and hang out pit boards. But there they are now, neatly in a row, the eight bins: four red, four blue. Williams are using crates to provide the required elevation, while Ferrari have opted for tyres.

■   ■   ■

The mood of restrained confidence is evident in the Benetton pit as first practice begins. The team are in no hurry to send out Michael Schumacher or Riccardo

Patrese, content instead to watch and wait as other cars sweep away hazardous surface dust. Patrese, his hands lost in his pockets, ambles across to the pit wall, soon to be followed by Schumacher. They are joined by Mika Hakkinen, the Finn given his chance with McLaren here following the departure of Michael Andretti. Seeing Schumacher and Hakkinen together, you sense you are glimpsing the future.

Frank Dernie, now on Patrese's car (Rory Byrne is back at the factory, working at options for next year's car, while Pat Symonds is on Schumacher's), reports to Brawn: 'It's still not cleaning up fast enough.'

Dernie joins a group of mechanics standing, arms folded, in front of Schumacher's car. He says: 'About 50 per cent of the track has been resurfaced and it's always pretty filthy here, anyway. It seems to come down with the rain. There's no point in going out yet. It's better to do 15 good laps than 23 on tyres impregnated with filth.'

The conversation switches to more fundamental matters, like the siting of the new toilets. 'You always need to know where the closest one is,' Frank reasons.

Schumacher, who appears to have made use of Dernie's practical information, returns to his perch at the pit wall. It is 10 o'clock, half an hour into the session, and still Benetton wait. Briatore, looking pensive, prowls the garage. At 10.05 Patrese makes the first move, striding towards his corner of the camp for his helmet. As he does so, neigh-

Mika Hakkinen looks in on the Benetton drivers

bours Senna and Hakkinen bring their cars into the daylight. Flavio holds back the perimeter tape to allow Schumacher into the garage and both Benetton drivers are ready for work.

They are into the usual routine. In... out... in... out. Each time a car returns, mechanics pounce, their hands working feverishly, while engineers scribble away at their pads. Flavio surveys all like some doting Godfather. An elegant woman photographer asks if she may take pictures inside the garage. He grants her request, then confides: 'But only because she is beautiful.'

Another run gives Schumacher P.3, but he is well down on the Williams pair. He is none too happy. The car is not handling as he would like, nor as he would have expected. He conveys his feelings to the engineers. Pople is by the car with his fuel cans, Kristan De Groot at the front with his spray and cloth polishing the nose. They have plenty of time now because a car has gone off and the session has been stopped. Schumacher climbs out and continues his discussion with Brawn and Jim Brett. The plan here is for Schumacher to use a 'Series VIII' engine today, and a 'VII' tomorrow, while Riccardo will have the 'VII' today and the 'VIII' tomorrow. The preference is to go with the 'VIII' for the race.

A truck rumbles past the front of the Benetton garage, carrying Aguri Suzuki's Footwork. Brawn shows Schumacher a full hand to indicate practice is to be resumed in five minutes. Television cameras close in to capture the German and his car drawing from the pits. Soon mechanics, lugging even heavier equipment, are pursuing him down the pit lane. He has stalled. Patrese is back in business with no dramas.

Cheesy Harriss sweeps the floor, others tinker at this, tidy that. There is constant activity. One of the passing figures in the pit lane is that of Leo Sayer, singer and racing fan. He peers in and continues on his way.

Schumacher returns with obvious concerns. Off comes the rear bodywork, in go the heads and hands. 'Looks like gearbox trouble,' whispers a mechanic. Brawn is on his haunches in conversation with the driver.

As Patrese comes back in, Kenny Handkammer gets Schumacher started again. Patrese is swiftly out again and mechanics check out the times. Schumacher is fifth, Patrese eighth. The atmosphere is beginning to change. Anxiety is filtering through the ranks. They should be strong here. This is where they are supposed to make the breakthrough. Something is seriously wrong. Benetton are off the pace.

Schumacher, in particular, is dissatisfied. He is attacking the track with typical determination, but he is having to fight the B193B. He is having to fight too much. Suddenly there are startled glances between team members. 'He's gone off,' says a mechanic, relaying the message he is receiving in his headphones. 'He was on a flyer, too. Only three-tenths of a second outside Prost's time.'

Driver and car are undamaged, but the portents are not good. Michael walks back, helmet in hand, assuring everyone: 'I'm all right.' A couple of minutes later the car is delivered by truck, a mechanic sitting on the nose to maintain the balance as it is lowered to the ground. His colleagues push it back into the garage, check it from all angles and brush gravel from the tyres. 'Looks okay,' says one, with obvious relief.

The basic problem, however, remains. Schumacher is still fifth at the end of qualifying, behind Prost, Hill, Senna and Hakkinen. Patrese is eighth. Schumacher says: 'We made some changes to the car for qualifying but they did not work out the way we had expected. McLaren is ahead of us, which has not been the case in recent weeks, so clearly there is something wrong with the car and we've got to work on that.'

Patrese is not satisfied with the grip he is achieving, yet feels he has a reasonable balance. Encouraged by that, the team decide to go with his active suspension mappings on Schumacher's car.

■　■　■

The glorious red glow of Saturday's dawn fails to throw fresh light on the mystery. Practice and qualifying condemn Schumacher to more torment and two more spins. He will start sixth on the grid, Patrese seventh. The order in front of them will be: Hill, Prost, Hakkinen, Senna, Alesi.

Michael's concern is etched deep into his face. 'We do not know what the problem is,' he says. 'The car is unpredictable. We have a long night ahead of us, working out the cause of the trouble.'

Schumacher cries off a sponsor's engagement to join his engineers on their vigil. Flavio will stand in. They pore over data in the hope of unravelling the problem. Michael leaves for his hotel at 11 o'clock, the last of the boys at two o'clock on Sunday morning. 'I went to sleep with data in my eyes,' Michael will say later.

The clocks go back an hour this race day morning, September 26, and rarely has the grace been more gratefully received. But do they have a solution to the dilemma? 'I don't know,' confesses Brawn. 'There's been a lot of head-scratching and a frank exchange of views. Riccardo is roughly where we expected but it's been a puzzle with Michael. The fact is, we just can't get his car to work. So, we've decided to go with the spare.'

Briatore, his coat collar up against a fresh morning breeze, is as frustrated as anyone, yet has become conditioned by the fickle nature of Formula One. The gravel in his voice even deeper at this early hour, he says: 'Sure, I thought we would be good here, but it is part of our business. Nobody's perfect. The more you develop the car, there is no guarantee you go in the right direction all the time. That's fortunate, because if everybody improves two tenths of a second a day, you end up with an aeroplane! We're not happy but it's the first time we've gone backwards in a long time. It's sport, it's human. You must accept that mistakes are possible.

Schumacher, shadowed by Weber (dark glasses), has final words with Symonds

But is he not desperately disappointed this season of hope and progress has not yet yielded a victory? 'This year, you know, I feel we have not had the luck, and that can change your life. Last year we always managed to get results, but this year has not been the same. With a little luck we might have won four races: Brazil, Monaco, Hungary and Belgium. But still, the team is in a strong position and in the end you have to say we have again improved. In this business it is very difficult to go on improving, but we have done this every year now for four, five years.

'I am confident for the future because the motivation is very high and because of the people here. I believe our team is completely different from all the others.

The atmosphere is different. People laugh and work very hard. Here it is not war. The people know they have a fantastic opportunity. They travel the world and they realise it is a privilege to have this kind of job. I believe the personality of our mechanics is different, it's special. I look in other garages and it is like somebody has just died. It is as if these people have such a dramatic job. My philosophy is that the way to work is with enthusiasm and humour. I guarantee, I can show you many sadder jobs than Formula One.'

Flavio is similarly unruffled by reports that McLaren, about to lose Senna, who in turn is lined up to replace the retiring Prost at Williams, covet the services of Schumacher. 'Everybody is interested in Michael but we have a contract with him for 1994 and 1995,' he replies, dismissively.

Benetton are no nearer making a decision on a second driver for next year and Briatore insists we should not necessarily read too much into the tests booked for several drivers. 'It is not a simple situation,' he says. 'Sure, when you can look back you might say it was a mistake to let Brundle go. He had a big disaster at the start with us last year and then had a very good season. I saw the opportunity to get Patrese, an Italian. It is human. And Patrese, now, is doing more as we expected. The trouble is nobody realises how fast Schumacher is. Anybody next to him has a problem. It is very difficult to make comparisons, but it would be difficult for anybody to push a guy like Schumacher. I'd like to see anybody against him in the same car. Maybe Senna could get close to him. It would be interesting.'

Flavio believes Schumacher is the embodiment of the new generation driver and is gracious enough to applaud the performance of Hakkinen. 'See what has happened with Hakkinen here. I think it's very encouraging. It is good to give opportunities to young drivers,' he says. 'And rather than pay someone a billion, trillion dollars, you get somebody to do the same job for less money. The young drivers are the future.'

Engine deals, too, will influence the fortunes of Benetton and their rivals in the seasons to come. Briatore is having further talks with Renault here and Dick Scammell, of Cosworth, is a conspicuous visitor to the Grand Prix. There have also been suggestions of a link with Peugeot, though they may be merely politically strategic leaks. Flavio says: 'We have to see what is the best opportunity for the future and the more information you have, the better the decision you make.'

■   ■   ■

Despite an indifferent warm-up session for Schumacher, the team are able to eliminate another software permutation and it is confirmed he will race the spare car. It still feels better than his race car. The German decides to stay in the garage area through lunchtime and will have his meal brought up to him. 'He wants to work with the engineers and have no distractions,' explains Willi Weber.

More changes are made for the race, but the team still cannot be sure they have made the right turn. Soon they will know. They can do no more. The troops are not despondent, but they do appear resigned to an afternoon in the shadows. Patrese squats at the back of his car, head in hands, seemingly in meditation. Perhaps he is praying. The team are in need of a little help from above.

Out on the grid, Schumacher looks relaxed enough, chatting to engineers. The call of nature comes right on cue, as much a part of the ritual as pulling on his helmet. He vaults the barrier (he does do that with disarming ease) and disappears as Briatore and Walkinshaw exchange some intelligence on Senna. Schumacher is intercepted by a television crew on his way back and gives a final interview before sliding into his cockpit.

Flavio goes around his men with words of encouragement and pats their backs. They retreat to the other side of the pit wall, and wait.

The cars flash by in a thunderous rush to the first corner. Alesi surprises them all with a daring manoeuvre on the outside and leads through the first corner. At the end of the first lap Senna is second, Hakkinen third, Prost fourth and Schumacher fifth. Patrese is eighth. Hill, having stalled at the start of the parade lap, must work his way from the back. His title hopes are virtually gone.

Joy and relief... we've done it

An engine failure puts Senna out of the contest and, finally, out of the Championship. Pit stops by Alesi and Hakkinen bring Schumacher up in the order to second. He has planned two tyre changes and comes in at the end of the 21st

Victory shower at last for Briatore and Schumacher... and the young hero basks in the glory

lap. The crew have him on his way again in 5.3 seconds. Now he charges. Patrese stops after 25 laps. The crew complete the job in 4.9 seconds. If they were weary and dejected, it is not showing.

Williams intend only one stop and Prost goes into the pits at the end of the 29th lap. Hill, now up to the front, stops next time round. Schumacher leads. His advantage over Prost, in second place, fluctuates according to the volume of traffic but the gap suddenly closes from seven seconds to nothing as the Benetton becomes stuck behind J. J. Lehto's Sauber. The Finn, believing he is racing Patrese rather than being lapped by Schumacher, resists for six laps before allowing the leaders through. Twenty laps remain. Surely he cannot hold the Frenchman. What is clear is that Michael must try to make it without a further pit stop. All he can do is go for it.

For lap after lap the team nervously wait for the two cars to come into sight, then stretch their necks to watch them down the main straight. Every time Prost attacks, Schumacher defends. The young man's composure under pressure is astonishing. It is tantalising stuff. The tension in the Benetton camp is almost unbearable. At last they come around that final corner and lunge towards the line. Schumacher has made it, by less than a second. It has been one of the season's great drives, the more so in the context of the weekend. An explosion of joy and relief hits him as he passes the Benetton crew.

On the podium Prost celebrates his fourth title and Schumacher the second win of his fledgling career. Few observers doubt there will be more wins and, indeed, Championship success, for the German in the future.

Michael says: 'When I think of all the problems we have had and how hard the team has worked it is fantastic that it ends like this. I have to thank them all. I did think I might lose the lead when I was held up by Lehto but I know how difficult it can be to see who is behind you. I can't make any bad comments about him and it all worked out all right.'

Schumacher has climbed to within a point of third-placed Senna in the Championship and, although Patrese has failed to finish, Benetton are now 12 points ahead of McLaren in the Constructors' standings.

■   ■   ■

Even in their hour of triumph, however, they look ahead. 'Only four days of testing to come this week,' says De Groot. Then it's Japan, then Australia, then another winter of testing and into another season. Always striving to improve. But don't be fooled. This victory will not be allowed to pass with sober indifference. 'I'm going to get seriously smashed tonight,' adds De Groot. He may not be alone.

INDEX